699

THE FONDAS

Gerald Cole and Wes Farrell

ST. MARTIN'S PRESS
NEW YORK

THE FONDAS. Copyright © 1984 by W.H. Allen & Co. Photographs
copyright © 1984 Wes Farrell. All rights reserved. Printed in Great Britain.
No part of this book may be used or reproduced in any manner whatsoever
without written permission except in the case of brief quotations embodied
in critical articles or reviews. For information, address St. Martin's Press,
175 Fifth Avenue, New York, N.Y. 10010.

Library of Congress Cataloging in Publication Data
Cole, Gerald.
    The Fondas.

1. Fonda, Henry, 1905–   . 2. Fonda, Jane, 1937–
3. Fonda, Peter, 1940–   . II. Farrell, Wes.   II. Title.
PN2287.F558C65   1985   791.43′028′0922   84–27558
ISBN 0–312–29759–9

First published in Great Britain by W.H. Allen & Co.

First U.S. Edition

10 9 8 7 6 5 4 3 2 1

ACKNOWLEDGEMENTS

The authors and publishers would like to thank the following for the use of
photographs:
American International Pictures Incorporated, Cinerama Releasing
Corporation, Columbia Pictures Industries Incorporated,
Metro-Goldwyn-Mayer Incorporated, NBC TV, Paramount Pictures
Corporation, RKO General Pictures, Twentieth Century Fox Film
Corporation, United Artists Corporation, United Press International
Incorporated, Universal Pictures, Warner Bros Incorporated.

Colour section: pages 1, 2 and 3 courtesy of Kobal Collection; page 4
courtesy of Rex Features.

Nebraska lies just north of the geographical dead centre of the United States. This is America's heartland, the level expanse of the Great Plains where buffalo roamed and the Sioux and the Pawnee waged unremitting warfare against each other and, latterly, against the pioneers whose wagon trains crawled westward along the Oregon Trail, the Old California Trail, the Old Salt Lake Trail and numerous others.

Today the buffalo herds and the warring Indians are gone and all that remains of the wagon trains are museum exhibits and the preserved ruts of wooden wheels in the rich black soil of the prairies. But Nebraska is still the middle of the mid-West, more than 1000 miles from the clutter and excitement of New York, and just as far from the futuristic glitter of the West Coast. The coastal cities and the world beyond mean less here than the virtues of the pioneers: the persistence to endure the dry, scalding summers and the savage, blizzard-strewn winters, the patience to watch the the wheat, maize and oats rise and the cattle and pigs fatten. Qualities of honesty and simplicity, direct dealing and plain speaking. And if the simplicity occasionally shades into naivety and the innate conservatism into blinkered reaction, it's a small price to pay for having tamed the wilderness, for having forged the spirit and the character that is quintessentially 'American'.

It is no great surprise, then, that the man who came to be described as 'the definitive American actor' whose 'way of speaking . . . is so especially his own that he represents to many people the true essence of America, a kind of synthesis of all the heroes of Mark Twain, Bret Harte, James Fenimore Cooper, Hawthorne, Poe and Irving' should have come from here.

Henry Jaynes Fonda was born on 16 May 1905 in the small town of Grand Island, Nebraska. The last Indian war had ended only fifteen years before, the horse and buggy was the most popular form of transport and wooden boards lined the sidewalks. He was the first son of William Brace Fonda, a jobbing printer, and Herberta Jaynes Fonda, a follower of Mary Baker Eddy and her newly founded sect of Christian Science. Six months after Henry's arrival the Fondas moved a hundred miles eastward to Omaha, the state's largest city, where Fonda Senior set up the W B Fonda Printing Company. Two sisters, Jayne and Harriet, soon completed the family.

But young Henry's American roots went further back than the mid-Western prairies. Fondas were among the first Dutch settlers of the New World, giving their name to the settlement they founded some one hundred and fifty miles north of New Amsterdam, in what is now upstate New York. That was early in the seventeenth century, but there was an even older and more tenuous link with America. The Fondas had originated from northern Italy, close by the city of Genoa, birthplace of Christopher Columbus, but political persecution had driven them to emigrate to Holland long before the explorer had first crossed the Atlantic.

Young Henry's early life was conventional, contented and largely unexceptional. Though the Fondas knew middle-class comfort, discipline was strictly enforced in the family circle – both moral and financial: when not at school or at camp Henry was expected to help out at the printing works. Habits of persistence, hard work and self-discipline were inculcated early and never left him. They were pioneer virtues, but there was a darker side to them, too, as the boy found out one evening in the autumn of 1919.

After a family dinner Henry's father drove him back to the Fonda works. From an upstairs window they watched a mob break into the courthouse opposite and drag out a young black man who had been accused of rape and incarcerated in the courthouse gaol earlier that day. Without preamble the negro was strung from a nearby lamp post and his body riddled with bullets.

'My father never said a word to me,' Fonda was to recall. 'He didn't preach. He didn't make a point, he just made sure I saw it.' Understandably the incident left an indelible impression on the teenager's mind.

As a boy he was bashful and modest – not least because of his small size, an oversight remedied abruptly by nature in his senior year at Omaha's Central High School when he shot to six foot and one and a half inches, and became even more self-conscious as a result. It was not the most auspicious characteristic for a prospective actor, but Henry's creative ambitions then lay in a different direction. Since having had a short story published in a local newspaper at the age of ten he had decided to become a writer. Accordingly, when he left high school in 1923, he began a course in journalism at the University of Minnesota in Minneapolis. Nebraska boasted its own university but, true to the independent traditions of the Fondas, Henry was expected to work his way through college – and the North-western Bell Telephone Company, which had its headquarters in Minneapolis, promised good prospects of employment.

The promise, however, proved more substantial than the reality. Henry could only find part-time employment with Bell and he was compelled to take a live-in job as a sports director of a settlement house – a local community and physical education centre, mainly catering for young people. The job was extremely demanding; when Henry wasn't working until 11.30 at night he would be travelling back and forth to the university campus, a good five miles across town. Inevitably his academic work suffered and by the end of his second year the strain had become too great. Exhausted, he dropped out of college and returned to Omaha.

It was an unsettled time. Family finances made a return to college impossible, there was no job in prospect and Henry's writing ambitions seemed to have come to a dead end. Then, toward the autumn of 1925, Mrs Fonda received a phone call from a friend.

The friend was Dorothy – 'Do' – Brando, the wife of a local businessman and a founder member of Omaha's Community Playhouse. With a new season about to start she was in need of a juvenile to play the part of Ricky in *You and I* by the American playwright Philip Barry. Henry was the right age and his lean, blue-eyed good looks had surfaced from the podginess of his early teens. His youthful self-consciousness, however, had not deserted him and with the greatest reluctance he auditioned with the Playhouse's director, Gregory Foley. To his astonishment Foley offered him the role on the spot. Henry was too embarrassed to turn it down.

Later, Fonda's memories of his first stage appearance were scant – he assumed he could not have been very good – but the theatre had begun to exert its influence over him. Acting might remain a hideously embarrassing activity but there was more than enough to interest him in every other aspect of theatrical life, from the supportive camaraderie of the company to helping out with props and scenery – he had had a strong artistic streak from childhood which was later to keep him in the business, during slack periods, as a talented scenic designer. It was to be three years before he would convince himself not only that he could act but that he could also earn a living in the profession: a steady, accumulative process that was to become characteristic of his career.

In that time he would have the enthusiastic encouragement of Gregory Foley and Do Brando – useful practice for the woman whose then baby son, Marlon, was to achieve no small acting success of his own. Henry's family, however, was a different proposition. William and Herberta could appreciate that the stage might have attractions for a young man, but taking it seriously did not accord with either of their philosophies. When Henry finished his first season at the Playhouse in May 1926 he was strongly advised to seek steady employment. He found it as a filing clerk with the Retail Credit Company of Omaha – at a generous thirty dollars a week.

The work was far from inspiring and when Gregory Foley rang one day to announce that the Playhouse's new season would open with a recent Broadway success, *Merton of the Movies*, and that he wanted Henry to play the lead, Fonda's immediate response was to throw up his job and accept. William Fonda's reaction was just as swift: he exploded. Giving up a well-paying job with prospects to go play-acting was madness. Eventually Herberta negotiated a compromise; Henry would keep his job and rehearse for *Merton* in the evenings and on weekends, but for six weeks father and son refused to speak to each other.

Henry's apparently uncharacteristic change of heart with regard to stage performance wasn't due solely to boredom with his clerking job. Sometime during 1926 he had come to realise the true nature of acting – and how it could benefit him. In a conversation with his biographer, Howard Teichmann, he would later tie that realisation to a specific moment – the opening night of *Merton*: 'The short hair on the back of my neck felt like live wires and my skin tingled. That was the first time I realised what acting meant. It also dawned on me that for a self-doubting man, this was the answer. Writers give you words and you can become another person.' For a man who was also to admit, 'I don't really like myself; never have', acting provided him with a mask of universal acceptability, and even adulation. It certainly did on the opening night of *Merton*. The performance ended in a standing ovation, followed by a rave review in the local newspaper. Despite the arguments at home the Fonda family attended and when Henry returned to the living room that night his mother and two sisters sang his praises. His father, however, remained silent behind his evening paper – until Henry's sister Harriet ventured a small note of criticism. Instantly William Fonda's newspaper dropped. 'Shut up,' he snapped. 'He was perfect.' Henry was to recall that comment as the best notice he ever received.

Merton was a good augury in other ways. The play, by George S Kaufman and Marc Connelly, was the story of a naive young clerk in a small town general store who dreams of becoming a Hollywood star. 'Oh God,' went one of Henry's lines, 'make me a good movie actor. Make me one of the best.'

But the exhilaration of his first stage success did not go to his head. Before the end of the play's week-long run he was telling an interviewer from his old school's newspaper: 'I don't intend to make acting my profession; it is just my hobby. It was thrilling at first, but the glamour has worn off. From 7.30 am to 7.30 pm I am a businessman.' Words that would have cheered Fonda Senior's heart, but how seriously Fonda Junior meant them is a matter of doubt. Certainly he continued his clerking job until the following spring, but when a wealthy Omaha dowager suggested that Henry might like to go to Princeton, New Jersey and drive her over-indulged student son home – with a visit to Broadway and all expenses thrown in – he leapt at the chance. In six days Henry sat spellbound through nine plays, featuring some of the leading stage actors of the time. He returned to Omaha to the offer of a job as Gregory Foley's assistant at the Playhouse at a salary of $500 a season – something of a drop from his wage at the Retail Credit Company, but Henry accepted it eagerly, supplementing his income with a variety of temporary jobs in town.

In the year that followed – 1927 – he made his second important discovery about acting: not only did he enjoy it more than anything else, he could also earn money at it.

The opportunity came through an ex-Hollywood carpenter named George A Billings. Billings' principal claim to fame was an astonishing resemblance to Abraham Lincoln – a happy accident which had caused him to become the star of a successful silent movie on the late president two years previously. Since then Billings had earned his living on an indefinitely extended theatre tour, impersonating Honest Abe and delivering his most notable speeches. In 1927 he visited Omaha, met Henry and confided that for some time he had been planning a double act with a second actor impersonating Lincoln's personal secretary. Physically, Henry fitted the part. Fonda hurriedly revived his neglected writing skills and cobbled together a fifteen-minute sketch. Billings was delighted with the result and offered the young actor the role at a weekly wage of $100.

They set off on a tour of the mid-West which lasted three months. It would have lasted longer but Billings' second great talent was an almost unlimited capacity for alcohol. After a number of embarrassing non-appearances by the star of the show, Henry decided he had had enough, but his unprecedented salary had provided him with a sizeable nest egg. He had conquered Omaha and he had glimpsed Broadway. It was time to move on to a wider stage and so, in June 1928, after completing another season at the Playhouse, he did exactly that.

11

HENRY WAS by now well enough up on the ways of New York theatre to know that summer was a slack period for Broadway; auditions did not begin seriously until the new season in the autumn. However, there was an alternative in summer stock: repertory companies, which often featured experienced Broadway actors, operating in small towns or resorts. Connecticut's Cape Cod, barely 200 miles from New York City, boasted several, the most famous being the Provincetown Playhouse at the very tip of the cape.

With $100 in his pocket and a lift from a family friend, Henry made straight for it. Swallowing his nervousness, he asked at the box office about the possibility of work – only to realise his first mistake: the theatre cast only in New York, and had no vacancies anyway. He got the same story at the Cape Playhouse in Dennis at the opposite end of the cape. His confidence shaken, Henry retired to the nearest boarding house. The following morning he woke to find that he had unwittingly chosen the acting company's lodgings. His request for work had been reconsidered overnight: he was offered a job as third assistant stage manager – with free room and board but no salary.

Third ASM was the very lowest step on the theatrical ladder and it would be six long, hard and sometimes despairing years before Fonda would achieve the success he had set his heart on. Temperamentally he was well suited to such an arduous slog but his first few weeks at Dennis required some swift mental readjustment. It was his first experience of an established and highly professional company with a high proportion of Broadway veterans. Even the smallest bit part player seemed infinitely more polished and knowledgeable than the one-time star of the Omaha Community Playhouse.

The main advantage of summer stock for a newcomer was its rapid turnover of actors and Fonda soon earned his break – playing the juvenile lead in a play called *The Barker* by Kenyon Nicholson. The role won him a letter of introduction from a leading member of the company to a Broadway producer. But that proved to be the zenith of his achievements at Dennis. He was swiftly returned to the necessary but menial tasks of a third ASM.

It was at this time that a friend from Omaha paid him a visit. Bernie Hanighen was then a student at Harvard and had connections with a group of well-heeled Harvard and Princeton undergraduates who had decided to set up their own theatre company. Called the University Players Guild, it had just opened shop in a cinema at Falmouth some twenty miles down the coast from Dennis. Bernie persuaded Henry to drive over with him and see a show. The visit proved memorable.

The UPG were staging a farce by George Kelly called *The Torchbearers* and the performance was plainly not going very well, until the entrance of a young, second-year Princeton student named Joshua Logan. Destined to become one of America's top theatre directors and producers, Logan played the part of Huxley Hossefrosse, an absurd old man, for whom he had devised what he described as 'a flat, human capon voice which I thought hilarious'. Henry Fonda plainly shared his opinion. In his autobiography, *Josh*, Logan told what happened next: 'The moment I spoke my first line a high, strangulated sob came from the darkness. I thought someone was having an asthmatic attack. I said my second line and the wail came out again, higher and flatter this time. Some odd human animal out there found me funny. And, to my delight, it was infecting the audience. That night I had my first triumph, but whose mad laughter had helped it along?'

It was, of course, Henry's. After the play Bernie Hanighen took him round to the dressing room. Logan recalled their meeting: 'Standing in the doorway was a tall, lean man in his early twenties. His head jutted forward over a concave chest and a protruding abdomen which made him seem to lead with his crotch. He wore skimpy, white plus-four knickers, long black socks and black shoes. Either he had a daring tailor or he just didn't care. I was to find out it was the latter. His extraordinarily handsome, almost beautiful face and huge innocent eyes, combined with that roughhewn physique, made for a startling effect.

'He was looking at me as though he were about to pop. "You were Huxley Hossefrosse, weren't you?"

'"Yes," I answered, and he exploded with that same strangled sob laugh I'd heard all evening. At that moment I knew I would care for him the rest of my life. There's no one as endearing as one you can make laugh.'

Henry went on to a cast party where Logan developed his Hossefrosse impersonation, turning him into a poker-faced scientific lecturer spouting increasingly ridiculous nonsense. Henry responded with 'Elmer' – a comic character he had devised back in Omaha. Elmer was a shy, ten-year-old idiot who did fish impressions with his fingers. He was an immediate hit and promptly invited to join the company – for five dollars a week with room and board included. Henry returned to Dennis only to say thank you, goodbye and to pick up his few belongings.

On the face of it he was an unlikely recruit to the UPG. Not only was he three or four years older than most of the company – though he did not look it – he was from a very different social background. The UPG's leading light, Charlie Leatherbee, was the grandson of a wealthy plumbing fixture manufacturer and the stepson of the Czech statesman, Jan Masaryk. Male company members lived on board a 110-foot ex-World War One submarine chaser belonging to Leatherbee's grandfather and moored in Falmouth harbour, rehearsals took place in a hut in the grounds of a summer mansion owned by Leatherbee's mother. Other founder members included Bretaigne Windust, a Princetonian who had been born in Paris and educated in England, and Johnny Swope, another Harvard man, whose father was president of General Electric. Girls from prestigious colleges like Vassar, Radcliffe and Barnard contributed the female talent.

The company had been founded with the intention of giving student actors and actresses the chance to make up for their 'lost' four years of academic study. Though they aimed for the highest professional standards, they were organised on lines the Cape Playhouse company would never have tolerated. There were no leaders, no final arbiters; everyone had the right to do what they wanted, as long as they managed to convince enough of their fellows that it was a good idea. The result was not untypical of most undergraduate drama groups – a near constant ferment of passion, inspiration and fierce personal ambition, accompanied by outbursts of unrestrained adulation and utterly ruthless criticism. It was also highly creative.

In the four years that the University Players existed they were to provide a starting point for a quite disproportionate number of leading figures of stage and cinema. Apart from Fonda and Josh Logan, the company included future Hollywood stars like Margaret Sullavan and James Stewart, enduring character actors like Mildred Natwick, Kent Smith and Myron McCormick and leading Broadway directors like Bretaigne Windust, whose success came to rival Logan's.

His time with the UPG was Fonda's theatrical apprenticeship. As a repertory company their policy was to stage the widest range of popular theatre, from high melodrama to broad comedy, and Henry took his turn at each, soon establishing himself as the company's leading player. His beginnings, however, were not auspicious. Henry's first role was that of an elderly nobleman in a poetic drama set in fifteenth century Italy. Despite his family's Italian antecedents, his flat, mid-Western drawl was suited neither to Italian speech patterns nor to dramatic poetry. The part was a disaster and Fonda only managed to retain his place in the company by dint of his personal popularity and his undoubted talent for set design and scene painting. He redeemed himself with his next role – as a punch drunk prizefighter.

This part allowed him to demonstrate two of the most important aspects of his acting talent – his exceptional ability to project his own distinctively American heritage, and his total conviction. The highpoint of the play was a boxing match between Fonda and his co-star Johnny Swope; neither knew much about boxing but they rehearsed so extensively and with such enthusiasm that a member of the public, witnessing a rehearsal in a Falmouth alley, immediately called the police. On stage bloody noses were common. The play, and Henry, were a success.

'I soon realised,' Josh Logan wrote later, 'that he was a rather strange but special kind of leading man who could play romantic, sexually effective parts and still retain his "cool". He was always real, un-actory, and almost, but never quite, inaudible . . . Fonda has a concept of truth in the theatre that makes most of his peers seem pallid. He will never be seduced into overstating a point or a mood.'

Henry might have earned his place with the University Players, but Broadway was a different prospect. When the student actors returned to college in September, Fonda made his first foray into the New York acting world. With his innate sense of realism he did not expect things to be easy but his most pessimistic forecasts could not have prepared him for the reality. The first blow came with the letter of introduction to a Broadway producer which he had carefully hoarded from his short time at Dennis. It did not take him beyond the producer's secretary, chiefly because the actor who had penned it had unsuccessfully sought work from the same producer the day before.

Soon Henry was reduced to living on rice and water, consumed at the longest possible intervals between his endless rounds of agents' and producers' offices. 'I wasn't terribly smart,' he remembered. 'If I'd been smart, I would have given up and gone home. It never occurred to me to be discouraged.' It was just as well. Four more equally dismal winters awaited him.

At Christmas he was joined by University Player Kent Smith who had just been thrown out of Harvard for poor class attendance. Together they found their only acting work of the winter, performing in a National Junior Theatre production of *Twelfth Night* in Washington DC. Fonda played an unlikely Sir Andrew Aguecheek.

In April Henry received a telegram from Bernie Hanighen in Harvard. The university's dramatic club were staging a musical comedy, co-written by Hanighen, and there was a place for Henry's Elmer impersonation. In

16

the company was another outsider – Charlie Leatherbee's girlfriend, a petite, honey-haired eighteen-year-old with a husky voice and a whimsical yet magnetic personality. The daughter of a wealthy Virginia family, Margaret Sullavan was studying drama and dance while working in a local bookshop. She was as passionately dedicated to theatre, and as fiercely ambitious, as Fonda and her magnetism had an immediate effect on him – and most of the male cast.

When the University Players returned to Falmouth in June, Charlie Leatherbee insisted on bringing along 'Peggy' – as she preferred to be called. Artistically it was an astute move – Sullavan and Fonda, usually teamed together, became the UPG's most popular and successful actors. Personally it was a disaster. Henry and Peggy's chemistry proved just as lively offstage as it was on.

In many ways Fonda's first serious relationship set a pattern for the four major ones – all resulting in marriage – that followed it. Like the women who followed, Margaret Sullavan was vivacious and outgoing, more likely to be the pursuer than the pursued in any romantic entanglement. That chimed well with Fonda's characteristic reticence. As he was to admit to his biographer, 'I'm easily seduced.' But that willingness to let the woman take the initiative did not imply an easygoing or over-tolerant nature. The stubborn determination Fonda portrayed so feelingly on stage, and later on the screen, could be matched by a less appealing inflexibility in his private life – an inflexibility that could shade easily into intolerance and even an unwitting cruelty. His constant urge for perfection wasn't confined to his acting. Disagreements could turn into feuds – one with Josh Logan, involving his promotion over Fonda to a director of the UPG, lasted for over a year.

Margaret Sullavan, however, gave back as good as she got, contributing her own brand of wilful temperament; her tantrums, though, were explosive and short-lived. As a result her romance with Fonda was marked by a succession of blazing rows and tearful reconciliations. In terms of talent, ego and temperament, she was to come closest, of all his marital partners, to being Fonda's equal, and that was to drive them apart just as strongly as it bound them together. As with most close actor-actress relationships, there was a constant potential for discord in the simple fact that both were unlikely to achieve simultaneously the success that each craved.

In the winter of 1929–30 it seemed that Fonda would make his mark first. He won his first Broadway job, as a walk-on and understudy in a Theatre Guild production of *A Game of Love and Death* with Claude Rains. It was the play's misfortune, however, to open in the same month that Wall Street crashed, and it only lasted six weeks.

At the end of the next summer's UPG season it was Sullavan's turn to make good. She landed an understudy role in a touring version of a Broadway comedy hit, *Strictly Dishonourable* by Preston Sturges. This led swiftly to her first Broadway part – and some flattering notices – in an otherwise forgettable play called *A Modern Virgin*, which opened in May 1931. But she still managed to rejoin the University Players at Falmouth that summer and later in Baltimore where they were presenting their first winter season. It was there, on 25 December 1931, that she and Fonda were married, the wedding celebrations being interrupted by Henry's appearance in a matinee performance.

Fonda finished the Baltimore season and joined his wife in New York where she had a role in a new play. This undoubtedly rankled with the unemployed Fonda and their old arguments took on a renewed vigour. Within two months the marriage was over. Its failure – compounded by the knowledge that Sullavan swiftly stepped into an affair with a Broadway producer – threw Fonda into a depression as deep as that suffered by the entire country at that time. The only work he could find that summer was as a hired hand and scenic designer at a small theatre in Maine; even the University Players were denied to him – he had resigned from them on his marriage.

But 1932 also proved to be the UPG's final season. In the autumn three of its alumni – Josh Logan, Myron McCormick and a Princeton architectural graduate with few acting ambitions called James Stewart – followed Henry to New York. The four of them moved into a sleazy, two-room apartment on West 63rd Street in Manhattan. The rest of the building was tenanted by prostitutes; 'Legs' Diamond, the gangster, had his HQ in a hotel two doors away. The address lacked almost everything but local colour – Fonda immediately dubbed it the 'Casa Gangrene'.

The winter brought another walk-on and understudying role but the following summer found Henry back in scenic design, at the Westchester Theatre in Mount Kisco, New York. Dire necessity forced this job on him – Margaret Sullavan, now divorced from him, was playing leading roles at the theatre and she had just signed a Hollywood contract. They maintained a cool distance from each other.

The winter of 1933, however, saw an upturn in Henry's fortunes. He and Jimmy Stewart won roles in a short-lived Broadway play and in the following March Fonda finally achieved his New York breakthrough. It came, surprisingly, through a comedy role. A young impresario from Detroit named Leonard Sillman was producing a low-cost revue entitled *New Faces*, featuring unknown performers. Henry was signed on the strength of a comic pantomime involving a man attempting to change a baby's nappy while driving a car – a development of his joint party pieces with Josh Logan.

The show was a hit, with Fonda and another newcomer, Imogene Coca, a young classical dancer who, until then, had no inkling of her considerable comedy talent, being singled out for special praise by the critics. It might not have been the great dramatic role Henry had dreamed of but there was no doubt that he had arrived. Overnight the young actor who a few months before had only been able to get work as a scenic designer was in demand. Impresario Dwight Deere Wiman offered him $100 a week for one year plus dancing tuition in order to turn him into a musical comedy star. Leland Hayward, one of New York's leading agents, promised seven times that amount if Fonda would sign with him. Henry was still wondering how that heady sum could be earned when he received a three-page telegram from Hayward in Hollywood. A film contract with producer Walter Wanger was Henry's for the asking. Fonda telegraphed a one-word reply: 'No.'

His reasoning was simple. He wanted to be a top stage actor and Wiman's offer had given him the financial security to achieve this ambition – while Hollywood was 2,000 miles away from it. Implicit in his decision, too, was the stage actor's belief – even stronger then than it is now – that 'real' acting only took place on wooden boards before a live audience, not in front of an unresponsive camera lens. It was a belief that cut little ice with Leland Hayward. A swift and colourful phone call from California changed Fonda's mind. He flew out to the West Coast and found himself signing a contract to do two films a year, starting at $1,000 a week and with the opportunity to continue his stage work when he was not filming.

An astonished Fonda returned to the Westchester Theatre as a leading man in a production of Ferenc Molnar's *The Swan*. But 1934 had an even more spectacular surprise in store. Fonda's co-star in *The Swan* was an actor called Geoffrey Kerr. Kerr's wife, the actress June Walker, was due to appear in a new play co-written by Marc Connolly, author of *Merton of the Movies*, and the production urgently needed a male lead. When June Walker saw Fonda perform at Westchester she thought him ideal for the part. Marc Connolly visited Westchester and agreed, and Fonda was quickly recruited for the play that would make his name as a dramatic actor.

The Farmer Takes a Wife was a romantic tale set along New York State's Erie Canal in the mid-nineteenth century. Fonda's role – that of Dan Harrow – was the first of a strain that he would make peculiarly his own: a straightforward, even solid character, undemonstrative yet always dependable, masculine yet capable of sensitivity, utterly sincere and totally American. 'He had that gee-gosh, foot-dragging quality about him that Gary Cooper and a few others have always had,' commented Marc Connolly. 'But likeable, very American and very good.' His views were

echoed by the critics: 'a manly, modest performance in a style of captivating simplicity,' said The *New York Times*; 'an extraordinarily simple and lustrous characterisation,' added the *Brooklyn Eagle*.

The play ran for a respectable 104 performances and its closure only marked a new advance in Fonda's fortunes. The Fox Film Corporation – soon to become Twentieth Century-Fox – had bought the play as a vehicle for their current top female star, Janet Gaynor, winner of the first Best Actress Oscar in 1928. They had wanted either Gary Cooper or Joel McCrea to take the male lead, but both were unavailable. Walter Wanger persuaded them that Henry Fonda was the best alternative, and in March 1935 Fonda boarded a train to the West Coast. At the age of thirty he was entering the film industry as the lead in his very first picture and on an equal footing with one of Hollywood's best established stars. It was a remarkable achievement for a man who the previous summer 'couldn't get arrested as an actor'.

By any standards Fonda's rise to stardom was meteoric. *The Farmer Takes a Wife* placed him instantly among the front rank of Hollywood's most promising young romantic leads, actors like Robert Montgomery, Ray Milland and Gary Cooper whose own cinematic progress had been conventionally gradual.

Henry's introduction to the art and craft of screen acting was comparatively painless. He knew the role of Dan Harrow backwards and the fragmented, non-sequential process of film-making presented no immediate problems. His acting style, however, did. The film's director, Victor Fleming, who was later to take the directing credit for *Gone With the Wind*, pointed out to Fonda that he no longer had to play to the balcony. 'That's the biggest message I ever got in Hollywood,' Henry recalled. 'I just pulled it right back to reality because that lens and that microphone are doing all the projection you need. No sense in using too much voice, and you don't need any more expression on your face than you'd use in everyday life.'

It was all the adaptation Fonda's acting needed. Unwittingly he had created a style of deliberate underplaying, strict adherence to reality and an apparently unforced naturalness that was ideal for the searching lens of the film camera. On screen, as on stage, he appeared to do nothing, but the slightest change of expression – a sudden darkness in those clear blue eyes, the faintest creasing of the broad forehead – could speak volumes. It was an art shared by the cinema's leading performers, from Spencer Tracy to Alec Guinness, Gary Cooper to Clint Eastwood. And yet dozens of highly talented supporting players displaying the same quality have never been considered as stars. What did Fonda have that made the vital difference?

Undoubtedly his looks were crucial. His face was strikingly handsome, even beautiful, but its overtones of delicacy and sensitivity were kept well in check by a firm, slightly prognathous jawline and finely chiselled lips forever threatening to droop into grim melancholy. Innocence and imagination vied with passion and fierce determination. As the novelist John Steinbeck, who was later to become a firm friend, described it: 'His face is a picture of opposites in conflict.' More importantly, those oppositions – united with the directness and lack of pretension in his acting style – corresponded with the same oppositions in the typically American character: the character of the mid-Westerners among whom he had grown up; idealism was matched by native shrewdness, a passionate urge for self-determination by fair-mindedness and unflinching honesty. Whatever happened, he would face the world squarely on his own carefully thought out, plainly expressed terms. If you agreed with him, fine (only a bounder wouldn't); if you didn't, then keep well out of his way.

It was an idealised view of the American character, certainly, but it was, and remains, probably the purest and most attractive expression of the

noblest aspirations of that character. Not for nothing did Henry Fonda play more presidents than any other movie star.

The critics were quick to point out these qualities when *The Farmer Takes a Wife* was released. 'Mr Fonda,' wrote the *New York Herald Tribune*, 'is that rarity of the drama, a young man who can present naive charm and ingratiating simplicity in a characterisation and yet never fail to seem both manly and in full possession of his senses.' The *New York Times* lavished praise on his 'immensely winning simplicity'. The *New York Sun* declared that 'one of Mr Fonda's most outstanding assets is his appearance of sincerity'. No one doubted that in screen terms Fonda was more than a match for his well-established co-star, Janet Gaynor.

Certainly Hollywood didn't. Within weeks of finishing *Farmer*, Fox rushed him into another rustic tale, *Way Down East*. Gaynor was scheduled to play opposite Fonda once more, but either through illness or personal disagreement, backed out. She was replaced by a twenty-one-year-old newcomer, Rochelle Hudson, some eight years Gaynor's junior and with few of the latter's acting qualities. Perhaps Gaynor had read the script. The film – a re-make of a 1920 D W Griffith tear-jerking melodrama – was generally interpreted as unintentional comedy, with only Fonda's performance emerging unscathed by the critics.

The latter part of 1935 saw Fonda in his third film, *I Dream Too Much*, a romantic light comedy with operatic overtones. This apparent contradiction of Henry's two-films-a-year deal with Walter Wanger is explained – as it was, very quickly, to Fonda – by the producer's practice of lending out his contracted players to the major studios; the details were spelled out carefully in the small print and, although Fonda continued to be well paid for his performances, he had little choice about the type of film in which he appeared. As he was to comment later: 'I could name you twenty pictures without drawing a breath that I'm ashamed of.'

Whether *I Dream Too Much* would have been included in that number or not is uncertain, but it was certainly not one of Fonda's most memorable achievements. The film was built around the thirty-seven-year-old French operatic star, Lily Pons, then making her debut as a film actress. Columbia Pictures had recently achieved a notable success with opera-based films starring the soprano Grace Moore, and RKO-Radio – makers of *I Dream* – were anxious to emulate them. Fonda was plainly hired to give the best possible support to the untried screen actress and acquitted himself well: 'Such simplicity, directness and ability to create living character is a talent that cannot be analysed and certainly not dismissed as accidental,' rhapsodised the *New York American*. But Miss Pons proved to be a lightweight on screen and after two more unexceptional films returned to the opera stage.

Left: *Way Down East* Overleaf: *I Dream Too Much*

The following year Fonda made a further three films. The first, *Trail of* the *Lonesome Pine*, represented a return to rusticity for Fonda. Based on a popular 1908 novel, this tale of feuding Kentucky hillbillies had already been filmed twice, in 1916 and 1923, but it was given fresh life with a strong cast – including Sylvia Sidney, whose waif-like good looks had made her the archetypal Depression heroine, and a youthful Fred MacMurray – and technical innovation; *Trail* was the first Technicolor movie shot on location and its colourful evocation of woods and mountains proved a good crowd-puller. Fonda's portrayal of an idealistic and quick-tempered young mountain man once more successfully tapped his American roots. It was more than could be said for his next role.

'Screwball' comedies – bright, sophisticated tales chiefly characterised by the emancipated and occasionally slapstick relationship between hero and heroine – had been popular in Hollywood since the Oscar-winning success of *It Happened One Night* with Clark Gable and Claudette Colbert in 1934. It was inevitable that Walter Wanger would try the dependable Fonda in such a vehicle. *The Moon's Our Home* followed the unlikely romance of two international celebrities – he, an adventurer and writer, she a movie star – who meet, fall in love and marry without either realising the other's true identity. The film was well received but it was more notable – in personal as well as publicity terms – for its teaming of Fonda with his ex-wife Margaret Sullavan.

Since their divorce, Henry had showed no obvious desire to commit matrimony a second time. He had resumed the bachelor existence he had known in New York, sharing a number of rented houses with his University Players friend, James Stewart, who had signed a contract with Metro-Goldwyn-Mayer. They were joined by two more ex-UPG members, also trying their hands in Hollywood, Johnny Swope and Josh Logan. Despite a reluctance to become involved in the romantic gossip that passed for publicity in the movie capital, Fonda seems to have enjoyed himself, becoming a popular member of the film community; it was to be a paradox central to this reticent man's character that he could command affection and respect with such apparent ease from his fellow artists yet meet with overwhelming difficulties in his more intimate personal relationships.

Margaret Sullavan, too, had had her difficulties. A second marriage, to the director William Wyler, had gone sour and she had separated from him when she found herself once more acting opposite Fonda. It soon became obvious that the abrupt curtailment of their marriage had not destroyed all the emotions that had led up to it. Within weeks they were talking of setting up home together, but just as quickly the old arguments revived. Again it was Sullavan who made the break, but without rancour this time; their romance subsided into warm friendship, a transformation Henry accepted rather more philosophically than he might have expected.

In the event it was to prove just as well. After filming another and wholly

26

unremarkable comedy called *Spendthrift*, in which he appeared as a polo-playing playboy, he set sail for England in the early summer of 1936. He was to co-star in *Wings of the Morning*, Britain's first Technicolor movie. A complicated plot involved parallel romances between a gypsy princess and an Irish aristocrat in the nineteenth century, and their descendants in the twentieth, but the film's chief *raison d'être* was to introduce France's most popular young actress, Annabella, to English-speaking audiences. As in *I Dream Too Much* Henry was enlisted to provide solid support to a newcomer and to give the film American appeal. As it happened, the young French actress was quite capable of matching Fonda in terms of watchability, especially in such a frothy, romantic comedy. But Henry's first foreign excursion was to be memorable for private rather than professional reasons. During the shooting of interiors at Denham Studios, on the outskirts of London, a group of American tourists visited the set;

The Trail of the Lonesome Pine

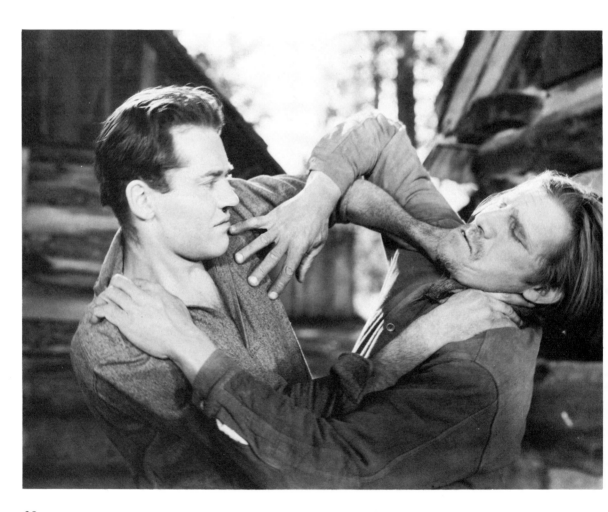

28

among them was a tall, striking, well-connected and extremely wealthy young widow. Her name was Frances Seymour Brokaw.

Frances Seymour's excellent social connections came through her paternal grandmother, linking her with some of New York's oldest, wealthiest and most prestigious families. Her ancestors could be traced back to a cousin of John Adams, America's second president, on one side, and on the other, rather more tenuously, to the English Tudor aristocracy.

Frances' wealth, however, had been earned very largely by her own efforts; her immediate family had known only an averagely comfortable, middle-class lifestyle. Ambitious and intelligent, Frances had left high school and headed straight for Wall Street with the twin ambitions of becoming a superb secretary and marrying a millionaire. She had succeeded in both. In January 1931, at the age of twenty-six, she married George Tuttle Brokaw, a newly divorced playboy, then in his late forties, alcoholic and estimated to be worth over thirty million dollars. Within five years he was dead. Frances was left with a four-year-old daughter and a fortune ravaged by the Wall Street Crash and Brokaw's profligate habits but still well in excess of a million dollars. As soon as the details of the estate were settled, she went on holiday to Europe, and met Henry Fonda.

Again it was the woman who made the running in the swiftly blossoming romance, and with such a witty, worldly and attractive admirer Henry needed little prompting. In a curious way their relationship mirrored Fonda and Sullavan's in *The Moon's Our Home*: Frances' knowledge of the cinema and theatre was minimal; Henry had little inkling of Frances' financial and social background. He had more when she invited him to join her in Berlin after *Wings* was finished. Together they travelled on to Munich, Budapest and Paris, by which time they were engaged. On 16 September 1936, barely three months after their first meeting, they were married in New York.

Superficially Frances appeared an ideal partner for the thirty-one-year-old film actor. She had good looks, charm and an incisive mind; her background represented a considerable social cachet for a boy who had grown up with no special advantages in Omaha, Nebraska; and her independent wealth ensured a smooth financial future, despite the fact that Fonda's own efforts were now earning him over $50,000 a year.

But the excitement of their whirlwind courtship papered over gaps in their relationship that were later to yawn wide, creating serious, and tragic, problems not only for themselves but for the whole of the Fonda clan they engendered. The wedding itself prefigured many of them in miniature.

Frances' sense of propriety was stylish but absolute. Accordingly the wedding became one of New York's premier social events that autumn, Rather to his dismay, Henry found himself having to wear top hat, tails and cravat for the ceremony at Christ Episcopal Church at the junction of Park Avenue and Sixtieth Street. Cheered by over 300 waiting fans, the couple moved on to a reception for 150 at the fashionable roof garden of the Hotel Pierre. For a man who less than three years previously had been subsisting on boiled rice, the wealth and social standing represented by the names of Frances' relatives was a little overpowering – but only for a short time. The wealthy talk most often of wealth, and its acquisition, which bored Fonda; social chitchat, unless it involved the theatre or cinema, bored him even more. Though he was happy to be civil to Frances' peers, he was even happier, the day after the wedding, to fly back to Hollywood to begin work on a new film.

Now it was Frances' turn to be bored. Fonda's friends were showbusiness people who talked shop almost exclusively, and Frances had no real interest in showbusiness. She preferred to discuss children, jewellery, the stock market, surgical operations or sex – a list compiled, with some unkindness, by Henry's closest companions. Generally, however, her wit, charm and impeccable sense of style – in a town which worshipped style without being entirely sure what it consisted of – ensured her popularity. She was on less sure ground in her private life.

Henry quickly established that acting was the main force in his life and his dedication to it, total. On a practical level that meant leaving home shortly after six most mornings to begin filming and returning late only to immerse himself in the following day's scenes. This routine was exacerbated in the early stages of a new role by a process Fonda called 'babying up': a gradual and constantly self-doubting advance into the heart and mind of the character he happened to be portraying. It reduced even further the low amount of energy he normally lavished on social and emotional relationships, making him withdrawn, irritable and generally difficult to live with.

Frances responded by concentrating on those aspects of their lives that they did share. She took over the management of Henry's financial affairs and involved him in the design of a house they planned to build on an isolated hillside plot in Brentwood to the south of Hollywood. She also became pregnant just over seven months after the wedding.

Like most first-time fathers-to-be, Henry was a little nervous at the news; he was not entirely sure if he were ready yet for such a responsibility, and, he confided to Josh Logan, he had rather hoped that the purely romantic side of his marriage might have lasted a year or two longer. He soon rallied, however, specifying a clause in his current contract that if labour began while he was filming he would have the right to break off and rush to his wife's bedside. In December 1937 Henry did exactly that, flying to New York where Frances had insisted on being attended by the obstetrician who had handled the birth of her first child.

On Sunday 21 December at Manhattan's luxurious Doctors' Hospital she gave birth, by Caesarian section, to a second daughter. The delighted parents decided to call the baby Jane Seymour Fonda – after Henry's middle name, and with a half-serious nod towards Frances' remote English ancestors who had included the short-lived Tudor queen. Her family nickname quickly became 'Lady Jane'; with such glamorous and well-heeled parents, promising an unusually secure future, it seemed entirely appropriate.

RE-MARRIAGE, and the prospect of fatherhood, had done nothing to diminish Fonda's appetite for work. On the contrary, even before Frances' announcement of her pregnancy, Henry was anxious to amass as much cash as he could in order to finance the couple's homebuilding project.

The film that had prevented the couple taking a honeymoon immediately after their New York wedding celebrations was *You Only Live Once*, another independent production by Walter Wanger. Made by the renowned German expatriate director, Fritz Lang, it was a sensitive and superbly atmospheric drama of a young ex-convict falsely convicted of murder who escapes from prison only to be killed by his pursuers within sight of freedom. It re-united Fonda with Sylvia Sidney, as the hero's equally luckless wife, and their performances earned high critical praise for their honesty and power. But such a harrowing and relentless tale proved too much for a mass audience and it was not a box office success.

Fonda moved on immediately to a three-film deal with Warner Bros, temporarily sacrificing the degree of choice over his roles that he had by now established with Wanger. This proved no great hardship with the first of the three films. *Slim* was an undemanding but effective celebration of the lives of linemen, with Henry as the ex-farm boy novice under the guidance of an old hand, Pat O'Brien. Fonda was later to include it among his favourites.

It was more than could be said for the follow-up. *That Certain Woman* starred Bette Davis, then twenty-nine, an Oscar winner and Warners' leading female contract star. She had built her reputation by alternating her screen persona between that of a bitchily ambitious woman succeeding against all the odds in a male-dominated world, and a more romantic, virtuous character generally disappointed in love. Her first film with Henry fitted the latter mould. She played a gangster's widow desperately trying to live down her dubious past while bringing up a young son alone. Fonda was her playboy lover who deserts her on their wedding night, largely at the instigation of his domineering father. Even Henry could do little with a part like this and his most favourable reviews offered deep sympathy. Undeterred by this reaction, Walter Wanger reclaimed Fonda briefly for another 'woman's picture'. *I Met My Love Again* featured another amorous widow returning after a ten-year sojourn with a writer in Paris to harass the more conventional lover she jilted, now a serious-minded college lecturer. The result was happier than the Davis vehicle but otherwise unexceptional.

Fonda's third attempt at a women-orientated movie, however, proved the most successful. Again he was paired with Bette Davis, this time in her capricious bitch guise. *Jezebel* was Warner Bros' attempt to pre-empt the anticipated success of *Gone With the Wind*, the film version of Margaret Mitchell's bestselling American Civil War novel. The Warner film gave Davis the opportunity to portray a tempestuous Southern belle on the lines of Mitchell's Scarlett O'Hara and she made the most of it, gaining her second Best Actress Academy Award. Fonda was her starchily proper banker fiancé, suffering her ill-considered attempts to make him jealous; he acquitted himself well, though, as he was quick to point out, the film belonged to Davis.

The conclusion of the three-picture deal with Warners did not mean an immediate let-up for Fonda, who quickly made another six films for a variety of production companies. He was by now one of Hollywood's most reliable young leading men, popular at the box office, hardworking and conscientious on the set and almost always capable of adding a depth of conviction and sincerity to the most unpromising material. His mid-Western virtues of innocence, determination and moral conviction shone through even in relatively lightweight roles, such as that of Don Ameche's assistant in *The Story of Alexander Graham Bell*, Barbara Stanwyck's foil in *The Mad Miss Manton* – another 'screwball' comedy, or in the heroic but otherwise undemanding role of a salmon fisherman in *Spawn of the North*, a melodramatic epic revelling in its authentic Alaskan setting. But Fonda had yet to find a director and a part to give the fullest resonance to the uniquely American quality of his talent, transforming him from a merely excellent actor into a towering figure in American cinema. That would have to wait until his first meeting with the director John Ford and Fonda's first role for him in *Young Mr Lincoln*, made in 1939.

In the meantime Henry's more interesting roles continued to prefigure his eventual transformation. *Blockade*, Henry's first film after the birth of Jane, began life as a Leftist denunciation of the horrors of the Spanish Civil War, then still being fought. Hollywood's stars were not encouraged to express political opinions by the studios to which most of them were contracted, but Fonda was an independent, both in his work and in his

Previous page: *That Certain Woman*, with Bette Davis
Right: *The Story of Alexander Graham Bell*
Overleaf: *Jezebel*

views. He avowed a number of liberal causes and his firsthand experience of Hitler's Germany had left him with a deep loathing of fascism. It was as much for political as dramatic reasons that he accepted the part of a Loyalist militiaman opposite Madeleine Carroll's reluctant Phalangist spy, but Hollywood's inevitable compromises soon diluted the script's original fervour. By the time the film was complete it was not only impossible to determine who was on which side but the very country where the story took place was in doubt. Nevertheless Henry was able to make a quiet but powerful plea against the indiscriminate slaughter of modern warfare – the first glimmering of his personification of America's liberal conscience.

Similar feelings ran through *Let Us Live*, in which Fonda played another wrongly imprisoned man – a taxi-driver mistakenly indentified as a murderer and saved from execution at the last moment. More significant

was *Jesse James*, a highly romanticised view of the famous outlaw, portrayed by Tyrone Power as a latter-day Robin Hood. Henry played his brother Frank as a laconic, tobacco-chewing farmboy convincingly transformed into a dangerous outlaw, and took all the acting honours. Surprisingly it was his first Western; unsurprisingly the most American of cinema genres fitted his dramatic skills like a glove. It was the first in a series of Western characterisations, relatively few in number compared to the bulk of his work but hugely memorable, setting him among the leading stars of the genre.

One of those stars – at the time a very new one – was John Wayne. The former bit-part player and 'B' film leading man leapt to stardom in 1939 as the hero of the classic Western *Stagecoach*, directed by John Ford. That year was to prove decisive for the careers of all three men.

The catalyst was Ford. A shambling bear of a man, dim-sighted, foul-mouthed and alcoholic (when not working), the Irish American director was the first major poet of the American cinema, stamping a distinctly personal style on his films in a way few other directors managed under the producer-dominated studio system of the day. He was already a respected film-maker, having won an Oscar for his direction of the moodily symbolic *The Informer* in 1935. But his lasting fame was to come with his depiction of America's past – a vision that was often naive and sentimental but at the same time deeply evocative and visually stunning.

1939 was the year in which Ford's artistry matured and that American vision first surfaced. It was a period of astonishing creativity, in which he made four remarkable films, starting with *Stagecoach* and culminating in his masterpiece *The Grapes of Wrath*. And Henry Fonda starred in three of them. Like John Wayne, he developed a special relationship with the director, each finding in the other a stimulus for the most exalted aspects of their respective talents. But Fonda's first reaction on being tested for the lead in Ford's *Young Mr Lincoln* was to turn down the part.

Something of a Lincoln fanatic since his stage act with George Billings, Henry had been happy to screen test for the role. Make-up and costume turned him into an impressive facsimile of the president-to-be, but hearing his own voice issue from a figure Fonda considered to be a national monument appalled him. Playing him would seem like sacrilege. It was Ford who changed his mind, summoning the young actor (the director was ten years his senior) and introducing himself in characteristic fashion: 'What the fuck is all this shit about you not wanting to play this picture? You think Lincoln's a great fucking Emancipator? He's a young, jack-legged lawyer from Springfield, for Chrissake.' 'He shamed me into it,' Fonda recalled.

The story of *Young Mr Lincoln* was loosely episodic and almost trite – a young, self-taught lawyer in small-town America of the early 1800s defends two brothers from a false charge of murder, wins a rail-splitting contest and a tug-of-war, courts a young woman who subsequently dies and stands for political office. The film's success lay in the unique partnership between director and leading actor. Ford united the disparate elements of the plot into a lovingly detailed evocation of early America, its people and its

Below: *Drums Along the Mohawk*
Right: *Let Us Live*

budding democracy, suggesting not only the principles for which the future president stood but the as yet undisclosed destiny of the man himself. Fonda simply *was* that man. He embodied Lincoln's warmth and modesty, his shrewdness and wit, his honesty and courage, his respect for the law and even greater respect for the people it protected. It was a definitive portrayal, as the enthusiastic critics were swift to point out.

Henry found working with Ford a joy. 'Pappy', as he was nicknamed, might be an autocrat on the set, rarely discussing roles with his actors and inclined to be merciless to anyone who incurred his displeasure, but his inventiveness and his sure instinct for knowing when and how to get the best out of a performance endeared him to the young star. He had no qualms about joining the director in a remote area of Utah for the location shooting of *Drums Along the Mohawk*.

This was another pre-Western, set during the American War of Independence in the Mohawk Valley, close to where Henry's Dutch ancestors had originally settled. The plot revolved around a series of skirmishes between early homesteaders and local Indians. Once more Ford transformed what could easily have been a conventional costume drama into a richly evocative portrait of early American life, giving Fonda the opportunity to score again – particularly in a scene of quiet power where he describes the horror of an unseen battle.

Ford's next film offered a role which Henry would have happily sold his soul to play, and virtually did. The film was the screen version of John Steinbeck's *The Grapes of Wrath*, the saga of the share-cropping Joad family, evicted from the dust bowl of Oklahoma by nameless corporations and forced to journey West in search of work. It was the story of America's 'Okies', the half-forgotten victims of the Depression.

Henry had long been admirer of Steinbeck and this story chimed exactly with his political convictions. Even more important, the leading role of Tom Joad, the family's elder son whose passionate sense of justice turns him into both a political activist and an outlaw, was precisely tailored to his talents. Unfortunately Darryl F Zanuck, the hard-nosed production chief of Twentieth Century-Fox who were making the film, was also aware of this. Fonda won the part that would immortalise his talents by signing a seven-year contract with Fox – a move he was to regret bitterly.

At the time, however, it seemed a bearable exchange. Shot in sharply etched, documentary style by Gregg Toland – a director of photography new to Ford – the film had all the epic strength of Ford's previous work but none of its sentimentality. Today its impact remains undiluted – as a tragic tale of simple, decent farming folk, as a deeply evocative portrait of a neglected area of modern America, and as a devastating indictment of a genuine social injustice; it was one of the few occasions on which Hollywood allowed itself to face such issues head on, and with a radical

Previous page: *The Grapes of Wrath*

stance – adopted from the novel – that would still be astonishing in a major studio today. And at the film's heart was Henry Fonda. His Tom Joad was a young man of simple truths and burning honesty, fundamentally decent but passionate enough to defend his well-developed sense of personal morality and honour (he has no regrets about flattening the head 'plumb to squash' of a dance hall brawler who knifed him and his retaliation when a company guard kills a striking Okie friend is swift and murderous). His portrayal is both a superbly rounded characterisation and a symbol of the American spirit: straightforward, shrewd and land-loving, honest and law-abiding when the law and society act fairly, independent enough to strike out when they do not – a capsule embodiment of America's own revolutionary past. But it was in the film's climactic, and greatest scene, when Tom is forced to flee his family and haltingly explains his new political awareness to Ma Joad (Jane Darwell), that he takes on the mantle of America's liberal conscience: 'Maybe it's like Casey says – a fellow ain't got a soul of his own, just a little piece of a big soul, the one big soul that belongs to everybody. Then . . .' 'Then what, Tommy?' Ma asks. 'Then it don't matter. I'll be all round in the dark. I'll be everywhere, wherever you can look. Wherever there's a fight so hungry people can eat, I'll be there. Wherever there's a cop beatin' up a guy, I'll be there. I'll be in the way guys yell when they're mad. I'll be in the way kids laugh when they're hungry and they know supper's ready. An' when the people are eatin' the stuff they raise, livin' in the houses they build, I'll be there too.'

The Grapes of Wrath opened on 25 January 1940 to enormous critical and popular acclaim and went on to win another Oscar for Ford as director and a Best Supporting Actress award for Jane Darwell's Ma Joad. Fonda was nominated for Best Actor but was pipped at the post by his friend James Stewart in *The Philadelphia Story*. Henry, who never professed any great respect for the Academy Award system, consoled himself, if consolation was necessary, with the birth of his second child, Peter, on 23 February.

Henry's successes of 1939 had enabled the Fondas to buy the nine-acre Brentwood plot they coveted and an architect began work on plans for a home in the design of a Pennsylvania Dutch farmhouse. In the meantime Fonda began to pay Zanuck's price for the Tom Joad role.

It consisted of a series of lightweight, generally undemanding roles in unremarkable scripts which did little to stretch Henry's talents. Either he was repeating his familiar farmboy guise for *Chad Hanna*, playing the conventional romantic leading man for films like *Lillian Russell* and *Wild Geese Calling* or a naive young man in *Rings on Her Fingers* and *The Magnificent Dope*. Of the films he was obliged to make at Fox only *The Return of Frank James* – a taut and moody Western directed by an unlikely Fritz Lang – showed any real distinction.

Overleaf: *The Return of Frank James*

Ironically the few memorable films he did make in this pre-war period came when he was loaned out to other companies. *The Lady Eve*, made for Paramount and written and directed by Preston Sturges – one of Hollywood's wittiest and most sophisticated satirists – was a highly successful comedy which allowed Fonda to display his neglected comic talents to great effect. So did *The Male Animal* for Warner Bros. Fox's naive young man roles were chiefly that studio's attempt to repeat Fonda's successes in this field.

Henry was genuinely pleased to do only one Fox film at this time, and he had to fight tooth and nail to get it. It was *The Ox-Bow Incident*, made by William Wellman, a 'serious' Western that examined the psychological cause and effect of a lynching in which three innocent men die. Henry's personal experience of a lynch mob at work would have ensured his interest but the principles on show in the starkly told drama accorded well with his own. Its shooting was preceded by long arguments with Darryl Zanuck, who was convinced – quite rightly as it turned out – that such a grim saga would not draw in the crowds. He gave in only after Fonda had agreed to take on *The Magnificent Dope*. Henry, however, also proved to be right about the film. It was a critical success and has since attained the status of a classic. Fonda, as an embittered commentator on the main action, made his own mark among some excellent ensemble performances when he read a letter from one of the lynched men to his wife. Yet again he was the voice of conscience, quietly powerful and utterly sincere.

THE FRUSTRATIONS Fonda suffered at Fox took their toll at home. Never one to share his deepest feelings with those closest to him, he withdrew further into his own reticence, giving vent to his dissatisfaction in bouts of moodiness, sudden tempers or long, long silences. Frances, too, made her withdrawal, giving more and more time to her business interests when she was not seeking medical help for her 'nerves'.

Like her husband, she was an individual of passion who did not indulge her feelings easily, not so much through any deep-seated psychological reason as background. The Seymours did things properly, or not at all. And that included bringing up children. As soon as they were able both Jane and Peter learned swiftly that there was a right way and a wrong way to do everything. If Frances herself wasn't on hand to remind them a succession of nurses, nannies and governesses were.

Frances' influence increased when on 24 August 1942, the day after finishing work on *The Ox-Bow Incident*, Henry quietly enlisted in the US Navy as an ordinary seaman. As he had explained to Frances, he had no wish to conduct the war Hollywood-style, acting out a conflict in which others were living and dying. However Hollywood, in the form of Darryl F Zanuck, was not to be so easily outmanoeuvred. Strings were pulled and Fonda found himself drafted back to Fox – to star in a swiftly made propaganda effort entitled *The Immortal Sergeant*. With that penance done, he went on through basic Navy training to quartermaster school, qualifying as signalman third class, before earning a swift commission as a lieutenant (junior grade). Even then his Hollywood past exerted its influence: he was ordered to the Navy Department in Washington to make training films. He objected vociferously and had a sympathetic hearing. After officer candidate school on Rhode Island, he opted for air combat intelligence and *Mister Roberts* was sent to the South Pacific, where he spent the remaining years of war.

Back at home Jane and Peter continued to grow up at 600 Tigertail Road, the Fondas' Brentwood home into which they had finally moved in 1941. Despite the restraints imposed by Frances, these early years came to be regarded by both as something of an idyll. Henry, a keen organic farmer, had cultivated most of the nine acres; there were chickens, rabbits and a donkey each for Jane and Peter; even the swimming pool had been designed to look like a farmyard pond. It was a cosseted upper middle-class lifestyle doubly divorced from the workaday reality of most of America by the peculiar circumstances of the Hollywood enclave. Jane's fellow pupils at the Brentwood Town and Country school – her first – were the offspring of stars like Gary Cooper and Laurence Olivier. The Fonda children's closest companions were the children of Margaret Sullavan, now married to Henry's first agent, Leland Hayward, who had moved to Brentwood shortly after the Fondas. Their daughters Brooke and Bridget and young son William were of similar ages to Jane and Peter, but their upbringing *The Immortal Sergeant*

48

mirrored their mother's still tempestuous nature. This unruly influence worried Frances even more than the continuing proximity of her husband's ex-wife (with whom she maintained cordial relations). Henry's attitude to Margaret was still one of affectionate friendship – and if Frances objected it was something she considered quite improper to bring into open discussion.

Her sense of right and wrong, acceptable and unacceptable behaviour rankled considerably with Henry when he returned from the war with a Bronze Star and a presidential citation. He had been content to indulge her during the first years of their marriage but his wartime experiences had changed his attitudes, making him both more mature and less tolerant. After the first heady months of celebration, Frances returned to her business interests and her hypochondria, Henry to his long silences.

Meanwhile Jane grew from a chubbily angelic toddler into an enthusiastic tomboy, swapping her 'Lady Jane' epithet for a more or less permanent cowboy outfit; by the age of eight she was a competent horsewoman. Her idol was her father, whose image she consciously copied, as much from his appearance in Westerns as from real life (Henry always dressed in casual, cowboy style at home). Peter joined in his sister's games but he had no great love for horses; he was small for his age and remained more closely under the influence of his mother who extended her hypochondriac fears to him. She became convinced that he was sickly – a belief Peter himself reinforced as an excuse to stay away from school, which he loathed. When her own fears of illness were finally substantiated and she went to Johns Hopkins Hospital in Baltimore for a hysterectomy (cancer was suspected), she took Peter along for extensive medical tests. He was found to be in normal health, but one particular examination, which involved sliding a probe up his backside, left mental scars lasting many years. It was a sign of the state of the Fonda marriage that Frances told Henry nothing of her impending surgery and waited until he was away on location before making her Baltimore trip. By the time he returned the operation was a *fait accompli*.

Fonda's resumption of his Hollywood career was not a prospect he viewed with any relish. He was keen to return to acting but preferably on the stage – his last theatrical appearance had been nine years before in an unmemorable Broadway production, *Blow Ye Winds*, which had lasted just thirty-six performances. However no interesting stageplays were on offer and he still owed films to Darryl F Zanuck.

Fonda kept Fox's production chief at bay until a project with his old mentor, John Ford, was ready for shooting. *My Darling Clementine* was Henry's fourth film with the director (he had provided the commentary for a brief documentary account of *The Battle of Midway* shot by Ford in 1942). A Western, it was in many ways a curious choice of subject for the director, featuring as it did the 1881 feud between the brothers Earp and the Clantons in Tombstone, Arizona, culminating in the legendary gunfight at the OK Corral. The story had been the inspiration of countless scripts since silent days and had been filmed as late as 1939 with Allan Dwan's *Frontier Marshal*. But Ford's odd choice of title, referring to Wyatt Earp's shyly hesitant romance with the young Tombstone resident, Clementine Carter, rather than the dramatic excitement of the climactic gun battle, indicated his highly individual approach. Like *Young Mr Lincoln* it proved to be an evocative portrait of frontier life, a careful balance of humour, high drama and poetic myth-making, constantly rooted in recognisable reality (Ford had earlier met the ageing Wyatt Earp and claimed to draw on the former marshal's recollections) but tapping a deep reservoir of nostalgia for half-forgotten pioneer virtues – virtues that, paradoxically, did not always chime with historical accuracy (despite his knowledge of the real Earp, Ford was quite happy to change the characters and details of the actual incident in order to fit in with his private vision). Ford's Earp was a typical Fordian hero – a loner, laconic and even shy, rebellious but fundamentally moral, slow to anger yet deeply impressive, and dangerous, when roused. It was a part made for Henry Fonda and he took full advantage of its opportunities. 'Through his quiet yet persuasive self-confidence – his delicious intonation of short words – he shows us an elemental character who is as real as the dirt on which he walks,' enthused Bosley Crowther of The *New York Times*. 'Mr Fonda's characterisation of a down-to-earth Westerner, free as air, is so persuasive that his Wyatt Earp becomes one of the great "Western" heroes,' added the *Christian Science Monitor*.

The critical plaudits were matched by box office success when Fox released the film as its main Christmas attraction for 1946. There was critical praise too for Fonda's next performance in *The Long Night* for RKO-Radio. A slow-paced melodrama directed by Anatole Litvak, it was the story of a murderer trapped by police in an apartment block and reliving, by flashback, the events that led to his slaying of his girlfriend's seducer, an unlikely stage magician played by Vincent Price. It was based on – and unfavourably compared to – *Le Jour Se Leve*, a 1939 classic French melodrama starring Jean Gabin.

Fonda followed this with another Ford film, *The Fugitive*. The director had just set up his own production company and took the opportunity to make one of his most personal and uncompromising films. Its source was Graham Greene's novel *The Power and the Glory*, about an alcoholic and adulterous priest pursued by the authorities in an anti-clerical period of the Mexican Revolution. The story appealed to Ford's ardent Roman Catholicism but the controversial character of its priestly hero created censorship problems. To avoid them, Ford and his scriptwriter Dudley Nichols reworked the plot into an updated allegory of Christ's Passion. The

Right: *The Fugitive*
Overleaf: *A Miracle Can Happen*

50

result was a starkly told melodrama, photographed in a striking if self-consciously artistic manner and overloaded with religious symbolism. Such a heavy-handed paean of praise to the Catholic Church had only a limited appeal to the mass audience and the film lost a great deal of money. Fonda gave solidity and conviction to the nameless hero's anguished struggle with his own pride (a much safer sin than adultery or alcoholism) but he was unhappy with the part, convinced that audiences would not accept him in such a role. He went ahead with it out of respect for Ford but regretted it afterwards. It was the first indication that the exceptionally creative collaboration between director and star was coming to an end. In future John Wayne would supplant Fonda as Ford's favoured Western hero.

Henry, meanwhile, finally concluded his deal with Zanuck by appearing in *Daisy Kenyon*, a 'woman's picture' of a kind that harked back to *That Certain Woman* and *I Met My Love Again*. He played Joan Crawford's worthy husband while she remained torn between home life and the blandishments of Dana Andrews, her married lover. It was a marginally superior soap opera, and Fonda was glad to move on to his next project, a portmanteau film entitled *A Miracle Can Happen*.

A string of short stories linked by the common theme of how a child had changed the various protagonists' lives, this film was the lightest froth, but it gave Henry the opportunity to appear for the first time on screen with his old friend James Stewart. In addition, both were allowed to choose the writer and director of their particular segment. They chose John Huston, maker of *The Maltese Falcon*, to direct and the celebrated American novelist John O'Hara to write the piece. As a result their segment, in which Fonda and Stewart played two free-spirited jazz musicians in pursuit of the same bathing beauty, was the lone high point of the film.

A sixth film for John Ford marked the end of an immediate post-war flurry of film-making for Henry, and the beginning of a seven-year absence from Hollywood. *Fort Apache* was another Western, the first of a series in which Ford recreated the frontier life of the US Cavalry, using it to explore concepts of honour and duty in the tight-knit military community. Fonda played against type as an arrogant, martinetish commanding officer, contemptuous of his Indian foe (treated, for once, as a worthy and honourable enemy) and obsessed with his own, strictly limited sense of honour. As a result he leads his troops into a Custer-style massacre in which he dies, only to have his reputation saved by his wiser and more pragmatic captain, John Wayne, for the sake of the regiment.

Fonda's portrayal of the misguided Colonel Tom Thursday was unusually straightforward with few of those sensitive touches he had employed previously to bring compassionate understanding to his less sympathetic roles. In many ways it was a more serious example of

52

53

miscasting than his role in *The Fugitive* and the acting honours, and the audience's sympathy, went to John Wayne.

With even his most fruitful Hollywood partnership becoming less satisfactory, Fonda was more anxious than ever to get back to his theatrical roots. In the spring of 1947 some news from an old friend in New York provided him with just such an opportunity.

Since joining Henry's bachelor abode on the West Coast, Josh Logan had had only moderate success in Hollywood, though he had co-directed Fonda in *I Met My Love Again*. Chastened, the young director had returned to New York and promptly scored a hit with a play called *On Borrowed Time* which established his reputation. More hits had followed, including the Irving Berlin musical *Annie Get Your Gun*, which marked Logan's return from war service. Then he was shown a copy of a first novel by a young   *Fort Apache*

writer called Tom Heggen. It was entitled *Mr Roberts*. 'Although it concerned the Navy in the Pacific,' Logan recalled in his autobiography, 'it was talking to me about *my* war, the boredom and idiocy of it, and I felt it was written with a poetic lucidity seldom found any more.' The story of the cargo ship *Reluctant*, purveyor of toothpaste and toilet paper 'from Apathy to Tedium with occasional side trips to Monotony and Ennui' struck Logan as the basis of a splendid stageplay. He contacted Heggen and the two began to collaborate. Independently, as they worked, both pictured one man as the play's eponymous hero, the *Reluctant's* popular, fair-minded executive officer, forever applying for transfer to a combat zone and forever being frustrated in his aim by the ship's pettily tyrannical captain. That man, as they discovered when they talked of casting, was Henry Fonda. Knowing Henry's film commitments, Logan suggested he come and hear the play read through anyway. On a trip to New York he did – and instantly agreed to star in it.

'One of the most beautiful things about the theatre for me,' Fonda said later, 'is that it's therapy. I don't have to be me. I've got the mask on. And *Roberts* was one of the best masks I ever had. I knew that I had something they'd like.' It had all the hallmarks of the one Broadway-conquering role, precisely suited to his talents and his acting style, that he had dreamed about on the stage of the Omaha Community Playhouse. Lieutenant (junior grade) Doug Roberts was decent, unassuming, genuinely democratic in his dealings with his men, and heroic in the sort of quiet, undemonstrative way that rarely produces headlines but which Henry understood intimately from his own war service. His story, moreover, had drama, pathos and a great deal of comedy.

On its first night at New York's Alvin Theatre on 19 February 1948, both Fonda's and Logan's judgement was vindicated totally. An audience sprinkled with theatrical celebrities stood on their seats and shouted for more. The critics followed suit with a series of rave reviews, all of them lavishing unstinted praise on Fonda's performance. Within days advance bookings were stretching into a second year.

Overnight Henry's frustrations with Hollywood – his tussles with Zanuck, the films that had brought him more shame than satisfaction – were forgotten. He was launched in one of the most successful plays in American theatrical history and his leading role would be as memorable, and as closely associated with him, as that of Tom Joad in *The Grapes of Wrath*.

Fonda's escape from Hollywood also meant an escape – though a more temporary one – from his family. Absence, however, did not measurably increase the fondness in his relationship with Frances. When at the beginning of the summer school holidays of 1948, she rented out 600 Tigertail Road and brought Jane and Peter east, the marriage continued its slow but inexorable downward spiral. Having lodged with Josh Logan and his wife Nedda in their Manhattan apartment for six months, Henry arranged the rental of a house in Greenwich, just over the Connecticut border and a forty-five-minute commuter journey from Grand Central Station. Frances had a sister and brother-in-law living there and her parents lived close by.

While Frances felt more at home in the affluent New England atmosphere of Greenwich, the children did not. They resented leaving their friends and the freedom of Tigertail; everyone here seemed starchily polite, never wore jeans or cowboy boots and spoke in an odd, clipped accent. Jane adjusted more quickly than her brother – mainly as a result of finding herself a centre of attention at the local Greenwich Academy; unlike Brentwood, celebrities' daughters were thin on the ground here. Peter's emotional transition took longer. 'I wrote "I hate the East" on the walls,' he recalled, 'and then my father would make me go round and erase it all. In those days I considered Greenwich the asshole of the world.' Both children were heartened by the arrival of Margaret Sullavan, now separated from Leland Hayward, and her children, who were enrolled at the same schools as the Fondas. To Frances it must have seemed that she would never throw off the shadow of Henry's first wife.

This, and the continuing remoteness of her husband, began to have its effect; her business work became obsessive, her vivacity shrank into *Mister Roberts* lethargy and depression. That autumn she entered a sanatorium in

Stockbridge, Massachusetts, emerged for Christmas and re-entered shortly afterwards. Frances' mother, Sophie, took over the day to day care of the children. Henry, for all the intense creative satisfaction of his work, found his emotional life a desert. Though he had reconciled himself to the fact of his unhappy marriage – a decision reinforced by the grim memory of his first divorce – he was ripe for a new relationship. It came in the form of the twenty-one-year-old stepdaughter of Oscar Hammerstein II, the lyric-writing half of the Rodgers and Hammerstein musical duo.

Susan Blanchard was tall, blonde and beautiful with a freshness and a generosity of spirit Henry had not experienced for many years. As usual it was she who made the running, dogging Fonda's dressing room, initially as one of a procession of admiring fans. With more reluctance than ever before – adultery was not easily tolerated by one with his mid-Western values – he allowed himself to be drawn closer to her. 'I almost reverted to my teenage personality,' he told his biographer. 'Back to Omaha morality, back to the Boy Scouts. It wasn't an adult romance. My marriage and my guilt kept us at a most respectable distance.'

Meanwhile Frances emerged once more from Stockbridge in time to attend the marriage of her daughter Pan and to accompany her and her new husband on a honeymoon trip to Europe. Shortly after Frances' return to America Henry asked her for a divorce. Rather to his surprise she appeared to agree with equanimity. 'The pressure I'd felt began to subside,' Fonda recalled. 'I had been honest with Frances, fair to my children, virtuous toward Susan, and, finally, honourable with myself.' That note of self-satisfaction owed more to wish fulfilment than reality: when Henry moved out to a one-room apartment in Manhattan a few days later, he left behind a wife in a state of mental turmoil. Frances was a woman in her early forties who had lost her husband to a girl half her age, whose life depended on her being the wife of Henry Fonda and whose upbringing did not allow the possibility of marital failure. Her fits of depression increased; she returned to Stockbridge for longer and longer periods. To a friend she confided that if she were insane Henry would not be able to divorce her.

In February 1950 that desperate wish came true when she suffered a complete mental collapse and was admitted to the Craig Sanatorium at Beacon in New York State. By the end of March it seemed that her condition had improved immeasurably: she was no longer depressed; there was talk of her returning home within a month or two. Then early on the morning of 14 April, her 42nd birthday, she carefully wrote out six notes, one to each of her children, one to her mother and one to her nurse, went into the bathroom of her suite and cut her throat with a small underarm razor.

Frances' suicide shattered Henry. He had his wish for freedom but at a price that blighted his life and the lives of his two children. After a brief funeral service in Beacon attended only by Henry and his mother-in-law, the two decided to hide the truth from Jane and Peter, informing them that their mother had died of a heart attack. Understandable as this may have been in the immediate circumstances, it only compounded the aura of repression and insecurity which characterised the Fonda family circle. Inevitably the children stumbled on the truth from other sources – Jane in a magazine article the following autumn, Peter from a newspaper cutting at the age of twenty; his sister had first told him when he was fifteen but he had not believed her. Henry coped with his grief and guilt in a wholly characteristic way: a combination of dogged determination and a retreat from reality. He adopted the mask of Doug Roberts and went on stage at the Alvin Theatre the evening after his wife's death.

The children reacted in different ways. Jane appeared to accept the news with a numbed calmness; she had not been close to her ailing mother for some time and had become convinced that Frances did not love her. Later, when she knew about the suicide, she felt a guilty responsibility by not having lived up to her mother's exacting standards. The effect was to make her increasingly dependent on her father's love and approval – neither of which he was capable of displaying openly. Peter, who had always been closer to his mother, refused to accept her death and he grew increasingly fractious and disturbed. When it became obvious that Henry was going to marry Susan Blanchard he was deeply upset and a form of revenge, conscious or unconscious, took place soon after the wedding in New York on 28 December 1950.

On New Year's Day Henry and his new wife flew to St John in the Virgin Islands for a two-week honeymoon. They had not been there a week when an urgent message summoned Fonda back to the States. Peter had been playing with an antique Civil War pistol at a private shooting range near Ossining, New York. In breaking open the gun to load it, it had discharged, shooting him in the stomach with a .22 bullet which tore his liver, went straight through a kidney and lodged close to his spine. Only the promptness of a chauffeur who rushed Peter to a local hospital and the skill of a resident surgeon who happened to be expert with gunshot wounds saved the ten-year-old's life. Later Peter would hint that the accident was not entirely accidental. 'I'm not sure if I was really trying to kill myself or not,' he said in an interview with *Playboy*, 'but I do recall that after I shot myself I didn't want to die. I was also very scared.'

If it was an attempt to gain his father's attention it certainly succeeded. Henry was at his son's bedside within hours, and stayed there almost continuously for the five days it took Peter's condition to stabilise. It was another week before his life was out of danger; another fortnight in hospital and a month's convalescence at home completed what his doctor described as 'a remarkable recovery'.

The incident frightened Henry – the possibility of two deaths in the family within less than a year seemed an insane price to pay for happiness. He resolved at once to devote more time and attention to his children, a resolution that was not obvious to Peter or Jane once the immediate crisis was over. 'I guess my father's remoteness had something to do with that incident,' Peter commented later. 'Now I see that the life of an actor is a very strange thing, and I can see how it interferes with raising children. But my father's nature is, or was, incommunicative.'

Certainly Fonda's work schedule did not help. In February 1951, with 1157 Broadway performances of *Mr Roberts* under his belt, Henry began a nine-month nationwide tour of the play, ending in Los Angeles. Here, he and Susan were joined by Jane and Peter when school broke up for the summer vacation. It was the children's first real opportunity to get to know their new 'mother'. The experience proved a happy one. Though still only twenty-one, Susan Blanchard took her familial responsibilities very seriously, spending long hours with the children when Henry was on stage. Peter revised his initially hostile attitude and was soon annoying the Seymours by insisting on calling Susan 'mother', Jane – now enduring the first pangs of adolescence and convinced she was over-tall and plain – warmed to her stepmother even more quickly 'Susan was my role model,' she was to say. 'She was incredibly charming, funny and outgoing. When I wanted to dress like her, she helped me dress like her. When I wanted to look like her, she helped me with that. She put in a lot of time with us, a lot of time. Thinking back, when I realise how young she was, I appreciate her even more.'

This newfound family solidarity was not, however, destined to last. As autumn approached Jane and Peter were due to return to school. Their grandmother, Sophie Seymour, who had taken over the running of their Greenwich home, was growing old and Henry was becoming deeply involved in a new play which would keep him out of New York. Boarding school was deemed the most sensible compromise: Peter went to the Fay School in Southborough, Massachusetts, Jane to the Emma Willard School for Girls at Troy, New York State.

Henry's new play was a dramatisation by the playwright Paul Osborn of John P Marquand's novel *Point Of No Return*, the story of an unhappy New York banker divorced from his small town origins. Leland Hayward, Fonda's former agent and the producer of *Mr Roberts*, was also to produce this and was so enthusiastic he succeeded in persuading Henry to invest money in the play, something the actor had never done before. But the euphoria only lasted until rehearsals began. Henry began to see serious flaws in the play. Characteristically he wasted no time in making his views known and the distinguished director Elia Kazan briefly replaced the play's original director. Fonda was still unhappy when the play had its Broadway debut at the Alvin Theatre and immediately became a hit. It ran for 364 performances in New York before touring, with equal success, for twelve months. Its popularity did not diminish in the least Fonda's misgivings – in fact quite the opposite – but he was at least working in the theatre, his first love, and avoiding Hollywood.

He had no such problems with his next play. Herman Wouk's *The Caine Mutiny Court Martial* provided Fonda with one of the most challenging and personally satisfying roles of his theatrical career. He played Barney Greenwald, the reluctant but successful defence lawyer of a US naval lieutenant accused of mutiny against his hyper-neurotic and ultimately deranged commanding officer, Captain Queeg.

The play's chief difficulty lay in its double climax: the emotional high point of Queeg's mental collapse – which is largely engineered by Greenwald and wins the lawyer's case – is immediately followed by a victory banquet at which Greenwald drunkenly expresses disgust at his own actions. This final scene makes the point of the story, but it demands virtually a complete reversal of the audience's sympathies, and the responsibility for that reversal rests solely on the actor playing Greenwald. It was a daunting task for anyone, but one which Henry relished.

Herman Wouk later recalled: 'Fonda once said to me that there was no way to play the banquet monologue, technically; he had to get himself to believe it, and play it as though it were happening, which he could only do a few nights each week. On those nights he ended up in tears, and the effect was explosive. But from night to night no audience could have told the difference. It always seemed brilliant.'

As in all Fonda's most memorable roles, the character of Greenwald displayed high moral values that corresponded closely with Henry's own. Furthermore the writing allowed the actor to express those values with maximum force – and without recourse to the bombast or sentimentality he loathed. Walter Kerr of the *New York Herald Tribune* was one of a battery of critics who lavished unanimous praise: 'As he offers his broken, stumbling but heart-felt version of a nation of Goebbelses getting ready to boil their Jewish mothers down to "useful soap", as he pays honour to the role the peacetime Navy has played in staving off that terrifying day, he casts a whole new emotional spell over the theatre. We are exhilarated by a ringing, rousing, thoroughly intelligible statement.'

With a third successive Broadway hit to his name Fonda's career seemed more remote from Hollywood than ever. He now owned a five-storey town house on East 74th Street, Jane and Peter were within easy travelling distance for the school holidays and his marriage to Susan Blanchard was sufficiently well-established to allow the adoption of an eight-week-old baby, Amy, in November 1953; the couple had been anxious to have children but Susan had proved unable to conceive. Significantly Henry appeared keen to take on a much closer paternal role than he had managed previously. 'I'd never had a chance to be a proper father to Jane or Peter when they were infants,' he said later. 'I hadn't been allowed to touch them. But, with Amy, I used to be the one who got up at five o'clock in the morning. I gave her the bottles and I burped her. I just had a ball!'

A single phone call from Leland Hayward succeeded in disrupting this New York routine instantly. Hayward was producing the film version of *Mr Roberts* for Warner Bros and he called to tell a disbelieving Fonda that he had won the leading role – under the direction of John Ford. Fonda's incredulity lay in the fact that he knew both William Holden and Marlon Brando were strongly favoured for the role; in addition Henry was aware that he was nearing fifty – some twenty years older than the intended age of Doug Roberts – and that after a seven-year absence from the screen, Hollywood no longer regarded him as an automatic box office draw. To be offered the chance to immortalise his most famous stage role – and with Ford – seemed a heaven-sent opportunity. He was even more delighted when he learned that his old mentor had insisted that Fonda, and only Fonda, could play the part.

Henry left the Broadway cast of *The Caine Mutiny Court Martial* on the last day of May 1954; in September he began filming on the Pacific island of Midway. But it soon became painfully obvious that the old Fonda-Ford creative magic no longer worked. There was an immediate clash of egos: Fonda now regarded the play as personal property – an attitude which had already prompted a quarrel with Josh Logan when the co-author/director had tightened up the play on its long touring run. He knew the text and how to perform it better than any man alive, including Ford. This was something the sixty-year-old director was not prepared to concede; age had not mellowed his autocratic working methods. In putting his own stamp on the film, he began to coarsen the comedy, discarding much of the subtlety which Henry, and Leland Hayward, saw as the meat of the story.

At the end of the first day's shooting Fonda's unhappiness was plain. He was summoned by Ford who demanded to know what was wrong. Henry began to tell him – but never finished. To his astonishment Ford leapt from his chair and swung a fist, knocking the actor off his feet. Apologies followed but from that point on, both the working relationship and the friendship were dead. Filming continued but for the first time Ford began to drink on the set: some two cases of beer a day. The situation soon became impossible and at the end of the location shooting Ford was discreetly hospitalised to dry out. He was replaced by the veteran director Mervyn Le Roy, whose credits included *Little Caesar*, which had turned

62

Edward G Robinson into a star, and *The Wizard of Oz*. His respect for *Mr Roberts* was as great as Fonda's and the story regained many of the qualities it had exhibited on stage. After the first cut Josh Logan was also brought in for some additional shooting and earned a screenplay credit as a result.

To Fonda the film was a wasted opportunity, a pale shadow of the stage play and a bitter personal disappointment. In every other way – critically and commercially – it was a triumph: nominated for an Academy Award as the best film, it won a Best Supporting Actor Award for the young Jack Lemmon as the *Reluctant's* ineptly lecherous Ensign Pulver. It also re-established Henry Fonda as a leading Hollywood name.

THE YEAR 1955 proved to be a significant one for the Fonda clan: a series of ups and downs which was to end on a distinctly downbeat note.

Henry's career continued to flourish. After appearing in an acclaimed television production of *The Petrified Forest* with Humphrey Bogart and Lauren Bacall, he was offered the role of Pierre in a film version of Tolstoy's *War and Peace* to be shot in Rome. On the home front, however, cracks were beginning to show in his marriage with Susan Blanchard. She had started her married life as 'your typical Japanese wife. I wanted to do everything to please him.' It became obvious that the shyness which had once so attracted her masked a much less appealing rigidity. As with Frances, Henry's frustrations at work – beginning with the filming of *Mr Roberts* – were taken out on his family. 'Hank repressed, repressed, repressed,' Susan was to comment, 'and when his anger broke out it was terrifying. Slowly it dawned on me that I had always been afraid of this man.'

The signs were painfully familiar to Jane, who graduated from Emma Willard in June. But the seventeen-year-old's unhappiness that summer was interrupted by a milestone in her own career. The Omaha Community Theatre, with which Henry's sister Harriet was still closely associated, was trying to raise funds for a new building. Henry agreed to appear as guest star in a production of Clifford Odets' *The Country Girl* – and Harriet suggested that Jane take an ingénue role. Henry was not keen. From the days at Tigertail he had tried to shield his children from his showbusiness world, partly in a vain desire to see them grow up 'normally' and partly to dissuade them from following in his footsteps – he had no wish for them to endure the kind of slogging and thankless apprenticeship he had known. Nevertheless both Jane and Peter had taken part in various school productions – though neither as yet had expressed any particular dramatic

The Wrong Man

ambition. Peter, now in secondary school at Westminster at Simsbury, Massachusetts, was busy rebelling against the school's strict and conservative regime. Jane was more interested in art and ballet.

When the Omaha offer came, however, she found the idea fun, and Henry acquiesced. He was surprised by his daughter's efforts, particularly her ability to cry on cue: 'I asked one of the stagehands to whack me around, to slap me hard, and that plus the terrifying fear and trembling I had of acting on the same stage with my father did the trick,' she later recalled. Jane was more impressed by the fact that it was the first time her father began to treat her as a responsible adult; in the theatre they were hesitantly starting to find a common language. As soon as the production was finished the entire family flew to Rome.

War and Peace was an international epic with an eventual running time of just under three and a half hours. Produced by Dino De Laurentiis, it was directed by the celebrated American film-maker King Vidor. There were difficulties from the beginning. Vidor had wanted Peter Ustinov for the part of Pierre. Fonda, who knew the book, was aware that he was physically unsuited to the role – the Tolstoy character was tubby, bespectacled and not particularly good-looking. Accordingly he adjusted his appearance with padding and spectacles. When De Laurentiis and his partner Carlo Ponti saw the result they 'went into shock', according to Henry. 'Their idea of Pierre was that he look as much like Rock Hudson as possible.'

Henry did what he could, surreptitiously restoring his spectacles whenever De Laurentiis was not around and suggesting the character's ungainliness by physical clumsiness. His performance was eventually to earn him the praise of *Time* magazine for giving 'the impression of being the only man in the huge cast who has read the book'. But the reviews were generally mixed and the acting honours went chiefly to Audrey Hepburn's Natasha.

Fonda's problems were exacerbated by the unprecedented length of the filming schedule – some four months in all. They brought his difficulties with Susan Blanchard to a head. 'There were no sharp arguments between us,' she said later, 'but there was a great festering within me. I couldn't be myself. I wanted to discuss problems with him, and he'd turn a deaf ear. He had an ability to avoid confrontations with me. . . I felt I was being smothered.' One evening she announced that she was flying home and would not be returning. It was the effective end of the marriage.

Henry felt angry and betrayed but he begged Susan to stay with him. 'I was ashamed as hell,' he said, 'that a guy with a solid background like mine kept screwing up his personal life.' Peter reacted the most openly. Distraught at this fresh break-up of the family he took to drinking huge quantities of local wine and wandering the Roman streets.

War and Peace, with Audrey Hepburn

66

Jane received the news more calmly, at least on the surface; she was still close to Susan and found her loyalties divided. It was a relief for her to return to the States that autumn to begin her first year at Vassar College, then something of a cross between an exclusive finishing school and the feminine equivalent of Harvard or Yale.

Peter, too, returned to Westminster and Henry found himself alone in Rome. Believing that the future of his marriage still hung in the balance, unhappy with his work and isolated by his meagre knowledge of Italian, he had little mental space for anything, especially romance, but his own problems. A young aristocratic Italian woman, however, thought otherwise. Afdera Franchetti was the daughter of a Venetian nobleman and explorer who had named his offspring after his numerous exotic excursions. 'Afdera' was an Ethiopian volcano – and the name proved remarkably apt. In 1955 she was twenty-three years old, a willowy, volatile young woman, highly feminine and with sensuous good looks. Fluent in six languages, including English, she was a popular member of what today would be called Rome's Jet Set. She met Fonda at a party given by her sister, Barone Lorian Franchetti (who was named, less inspiringly, after an Ethiopian swamp) for the cast of *War and Peace*. Like Frances Seymour and Susan Blanchard before her, she was immediately smitten, while Henry did nothing. A mutual interest in art began what Fonda regarded as a casual friendship. As Susan Blanchard's youthful high-spiritedness had once soothed the pain of his second marriage break-up, so Afdera's more sophisticated vivacity did the same for his third. 'Rebound, it's called,' Fonda was to recall. 'I was old enough and I should have been smart enough to stay away from Afdera, but she was a totally unpredictable and glamorous woman.'

By the time filming on *War and Peace* was finished – and plans for Henry's divorce began to go ahead – the relationship was far less casual: letters and phone calls were exchanged almost daily after his return to New York at the end of 1955 and his fourth, and most ill-conceived marriage was in the making.

Fonda was due back in America to start work on his next film, *The Wrong Man*, directed by Alfred Hitchcock. It was the true story of a New York musician mistakenly identified and put on trial as an armed robber, an ordeal that resulted in his wife's mental breakdown. The theme was a familiar one for Henry, who had played innocent men falsely accused before, but it was a curious choice for Hitchcock. The master of suspense filmed the story in semi-documentary style, using the actual locations of the original events and even some of the real-life individuals who had been involved. The viewpoint was wholly that of the accused man, building a Kafkaesque atmosphere in which everything and everyone seems to conspire to incriminate him. But the plodding emphasis on authenticity robbed the story of drama. Fonda's dazed and silently suffering hero won critical praise but the film was not one of his, or Hitchcock's, triumphs.

Henry followed it with a much more personal project. *Twelve Angry Men* started life as a television play. Its action was confined to a locked room in which an all-male jury debate the guilt or innocence of a young Puerto Rican accused of murdering his own father. At first only one juror – the unmistakable voice of liberal conscience – argues for the boy to be given the benefit of the doubt, revealing in the process the prejudices, spoken and unspoken, of his fellow jurors. By the end of the play he has convinced them all that the accused is probably not guilty.

When Henry saw the television play he was so keen to make a cinema version he agreed, for the first and only time in his career, to act as a co-producer as well, alongside the author Reginald Rose. The story appealed to Fonda in a number of ways: like *Grapes of Wrath* and *Ox-Bow Incident*, it said something he considered important, it was a taut and literate melodrama and it offered an excellent opportunity for good ensemble playing. Sidney Lumet, a young television drama director who had never worked in films before, was enlisted to direct. After extensive, stage-style rehearsal, which Henry insisted upon, the film was shot in just seventeen days and at $1,000 below its already unusually low budget of $350,000.

'Rose, Lumet and I realised we had something special when we saw the first rough cut,' Fonda said. 'We dreamed of putting it into a small East Side movie house, the kind that held a hundred people at the most, and we hoped that word of mouth would spread just as it had with Paddy Chayefsky's *Marty*.'

But the distributors, United Artists, had other ideas. Deeply impressed, they gave it a nationwide release in their biggest, most prestigious cinemas. The result was an immediate commercial flop, which convinced Fonda never to touch production again. Critically, however, the film achieved everything its makers hoped for it, winning prizes internationally and gaining a Best Film nomination for the 1957 Academy Awards.

Meanwhile Jane was enjoying some triumphs of her own. In the summer of 1956 Henry rented a house on Cape Cod so that he could spend time with his children. As a vacation job, Jane joined an apprentice group at the Dennis Playhouse, the same theatre where Henry's professional career had begun nearly thirty years before. In a short time she had her first role, the non-speaking part of a maid in a Restoration comedy. Henry went to see it and found himself regarding his daughter in a new light. 'Nobody knew who she was or that she was related to me,' he said later, 'but you could hear the audience react. Something physical happened to the people in that theatre. They sat up, they sucked in their breath, they straightened up in

Overleaf: *The Tin Star*, with Anthony Perkins

their seats. She had presence. You either have it or you don't have it, and Jane had it.'

True to his nature, however, he did not share this revelation with her. She gained an inkling, though, shortly afterwards when the theatre asked Henry to guest-star in a production of his former screen success, *The Male Animal*, with Jane in a minor role. In one scene Jane was required to storm off stage, slamming a door behind her, which was the cue for Henry's entrance. One night her exit was so impressive that Henry gazed after her in helpless admiration, quite forgetting to come on. 'The last time I went up in my lines was at the University Players twenty-five years before,' he remembered, 'when Margaret Sullavan came on in a seaweed brassiere.'

When the summer ended Henry flew to Hollywood to make *The Tin Star*, playing a laconic ex-sheriff turned bounty hunter who gives Anthony Perkins' youthful and inept lawman the benefit of his experience. Under the direction of Anthony Mann, the film boasted a full range of Western clichés but the pairing of Fonda and Perkins had humour and depth.

Throughout this time Henry's relationship with Afdera had been growing increasingly serious and press rumours of their impending marriage had began to circulate. The news did not improve matters within the family. At Westminster, Peter got into a slanging match with a master who told him, 'You're no good, like your father. Anyone who's been married as many times as he has and is getting married again is a son of a bitch!' The row marked the low point of a long period of mutual antipathy, which Peter drew to an abrupt conclusion by punching the man in the head. A conciliatory letter from Henry helped to smooth over the incident.

At Vassar Jane's emotional confusions were less obvious but no less real. Her father's marital behaviour seemed to make nonsense of the values he had always drummed into his children. She was attracted to acting both as a result of the talent she felt within herself and the closeness it had brought with her father during their time at Dennis. But her fear of failure – and Henry's apparent reluctance to reassure her – left her undecided. She said in an interview later: 'I was brought up where people didn't express what they really felt. You hid everything. You hid your fears and your sorrows and your pains and your joys and your physical desires. Consequently I was a zombie, living somebody else's image, and I didn't know who I was.'

On top of all this she discovered boys. The restrictions of life at Vassar, said to be a preparation for 'marriage, motherhood and menopause', began to oppress her. Her studies gave way to a frantic round of dating and socialising.

Neither Jane nor Peter took much pleasure in their father's fourth wedding which took place at the Fondas' New York home on 10 March 1957. The bright, butterfly-minded socialite whom Henry married seemed no substitute for the more sympathetic Susan Blanchard, something Afdera herself freely admitted: 'I wasn't a maternal woman.'

After the departure of the new Mr and Mrs Fonda on an extended European honeymoon, Peter's school problems came to a head. Threatened with expulsion, he called Jane at Vassar. She arrived to find him crawling around in shrubbery, drugged to the eyeballs with phenobarbitone. Understandably alarmed, she despatched him to his Aunt Harriet's in Omaha and Henry's sister arranged for a psychologist to examine him. To the family's astonishment, he was found to have an IQ in excess of 160, putting him in the genius class. This discovery enabled Peter to join the first year at the University of Omaha the following autumn.

The events that led up to it, however, had succeeded in disrupting a second of his father's honeymoons. During family consultations over Peter's future, Jane hit upon a means of escaping Vassar – by taking a year's sabbatical in Paris to study painting and French. On condition that she finish her second year at Vassar, and take her studies more seriously, Henry agreed. 'I went to Paris to be a painter,' she said later, 'but I lived there for six months and never opened my paints. I was nineteen, an age when you know you are not happy but you don't know why.'

She was certainly lonely during her first weeks in the French capital, but that changed when she met a small group of expatriate Americans centred on a literary quarterly called *Paris Review*. Its editor, George Plympton, a young and talented member of a wealthy New York family, introduced her to some of the leading lights of Parisian cultural life. Still relatively naive and unsophisticated, particularly in European terms, Jane was dazzled and soon resumed her Vassar dating habits. When Henry found out, the Parisian sojourn came to an abrupt end. And back in New York she found herself as restless as her father.

Henry's European honeymoon had been a round of endless Jet-Set parties, balls and dinners, an intense social whirl that left Fonda cold. 'Afdera's friends were as far from me as I could possibly get,' he would say later. 'I always felt they were just putting up with me. Afdera was their friend and I was almost like a consort. It was the craziest, most insane marriage anybody ever got into.'

When the honeymoon was over he plunged himself into work on a new Broadway play. William Gibson's *Two For the Seesaw* was the story of a middle-aged Omaha lawyer emerging from the wreck of his marriage with the help of a tough and eccentric young woman from the Bronx. But there were problems here, too. The girl's character was fully rounded and original, and it would later win a Tony Award for the twenty-six-year-old stage newcomer who played the role, an ex-Hollywood 'B' film actress called Anne Bancroft. Fonda, however, did not believe that the lawyer's character was anything like as fully developed. The playwright agreed and re-writes continued almost up to the play's first New York performance on 16 January 1958.

It was *Point of No Return* all over again. Henry found himself trapped in a commercial and critical hit from which he gained no professional satisfaction. As soon as his six-month contract was up, he flew to California to make two films for Twentieth Century-Fox: a Western entitled *Warlock* with unusually complex protagonists, and *The Man Who Understood Women*, a movie-making tale that hovered uneasily between satire and melodrama.

The summer of 1958, spent with the family in a rented house on Malibu Beach, was to prove crucial to Jane. Her main achievement on her return from Paris had been to avoid a third year at Vassar. She took classes in painting and music but found satisfaction in neither. Though a woman of

Warlock, with Dorothy Malone

independent means – thanks to her mother's will – the twenty-year-old's apparent indecision was not due to dilettantism. Two facets of her father's personality were beginning to surface in her: a determination to succeed and a fierce egotism. Both focused on the one activity in which she felt she could excel: acting.

'That was what I wanted to do more than anything else,' she was to say afterwards, 'so I spent a lot of time figuring out reasons why I shouldn't. It was selfish and egotistical, it gave no enjoyment, I wasn't pretty enough, and so on. The truth is, I was just afraid to try.'

Among their close neighbours at Malibu were the Strasbergs. Lee Strasberg, a diminutive, taciturn man in his late fifties, was the artistic director of New York's legendary Actors Studio and foremost teacher of the 'Method' school of acting, based on the work of the Russian theorist Constantin Stanislavski. Among the Studio's more notable alumni were Marlon Brando, James Dean, Rod Steiger, Paul Newman and a host of other stage and screen stars. Lee's daughter Susan, though barely twenty, was a successful Broadway actress herself. Jane had met her when she worked with Henry on a film called *Stage Struck* which he had recently completed in New York. This was a re-make of a Katharine Hepburn success of the thirties, *Morning Glory*, and Henry had taken part chiefly as a favour to its director, Sidney Lumet. Jane and Susan had begun a friendship which continued in California, and it was Susan who finally persuaded Jane to take the plunge into an acting career.

The obvious first move was to try for the Actors Studio. It was then massively oversubscribed but Lee Strasberg was beginning private lessons; he agreed to interview Jane on that basis, and to her delight accepted her. 'The only reason I took her,' he commented later, 'was her eyes. There was such panic in her eyes.' There was ample reason for it. Not only was it her first truly independent action, it also represented a challenge to the person whose respect and approval she needed above all others: her own father. She was treading on his ground, ground he had hitherto shown no desire to share. Even worse, simply by being his daughter, that challenge would have to be made in the glare of the fullest publicity. The consequences of failure could be appalling.

THE UNIQUENESS of the Fondas does not lie in their considerable individual talents or their peculiar 'star' qualities – every generation boasts its quota of acting luminaries. Neither does it lie in the fact that they all happen to be closely related – there are other equally renowned stage families. What does distinguish them is their remarkable ability to embody, both in their acting and in their own lives, values and aspirations that chime almost uncannily with the values and aspirations of the America they know and knew. In his performances in films like *Young Mr Lincoln*, *Grapes of Wrath* and *Twelve Angry Men*, and plays like *Mr Roberts* and *The Caine Mutiny Court Martial*, Henry united the rugged individualism of his country's pioneer past with the decency and compassion required by the more complex but still basically liberal present – even if that liberalism was tainted by the injustices of the Depression and Cold War anti-red scares. By his mid-fifties Fonda had taken on the stature of a national institution: 'the American symbol of the unbiased, uncorrupted man' as one critic put it.

Both Jane and Peter were now about to fulfil similar cultural functions. But the society they would reflect was no longer the relatively seamless fabric Henry had helped to define. It was richer, more complex and a lot less naive. The artistic compromise Henry had worked was yearly becoming harder to repeat. Revolution – political, cultural and sexual – was in the air, forcing individuals to choose sides whether they wanted to or not. It was ironic that as Jane's and then Peter's commitment to acting began to bridge the emotional divides of childhood the nature of their work should distance them even further from their father and everything he stood for.

Jane's entry into Lee Strasberg's private classes prefigured this conflict. Self-taught as he was, Henry was no great respecter of acting schools as such, and Strasberg's particular 'Method' seemed to him nonsensical and demeaning. Essentially it involved building a character from the inside, understanding his or her psychology by relating it to the actor's own. Pure technique received comparatively little emphasis.

In fact Henry's own practice of 'babying up' a new role was remarkably similar, but to his mind it was an instinctive, even mysterious process and bringing it under close critical analysis seemed to invite disaster. This is what appalled him most about Actors Studio practices. Every new student was obliged to perform an exercise in which he or she re-lived an intense emotional experience in front of Strasberg and fellow class members. The idea was for each individual to reveal their most profound emotions and inhibitions and so come to terms with them in a way which could later be used for dramatic performance. Psycho-analysis outside the classes was also encouraged.

Jane's first exercise was an ordeal she put off for several weeks and when it was over Strasberg's characteristically flat and unemotional criticism seemed a put-down. The congratulations of her fellow students – who were more familiar with their teacher's mode of expression – quickly reassured her. She had passed her first test with flying colours.

'My life changed radically within twenty-four hours,' she said later. 'It was just a night-and-day difference. Before, I'd been scared and extremely self-conscious. After that exercise I was somebody else. From then on I worked harder than anybody else. I was more ragged than anybody else. I was the rattiest, wannest, most straggle-haired.'

These were heady times for Jane. In a bid to establish her independence – and to avoid the relentless party atmosphere of the Afdera-dominated household – she moved out of the Fonda New York townhouse and into her own apartment, even if it was only two blocks away. She acquired an agent and, rather to her astonishment, began to support herself by fashion modelling: 'I thought I looked pretty,' she said, 'but not really beautiful.' A swift succession of national magazine covers did not really convince her otherwise. Undoubtedly the fact that she was Henry Fonda's daughter got her many more auditions than any other newcomer could rightfully have expected, but her looks – a blend of youthful innocence, sexiness and a sturdy coltishness derived from her tomboyish childhood – offered something new and appealing, she was also conscientious and very hardworking. These were all qualities that would prove useful in her dramatic career – which took off as meteorically as Henry's had done some twenty-five years before. Within months of beginning Strasberg's classes she was offered a seven-year contract for one film a year and the female lead in the film version of a bestselling novel called *Parrish*. Its producer/director was Henry's old friend Josh Logan, who planned to match Jane with another screen newcomer called Warren Beatty.

When the project fell through, Logan switched his two principals to a film entitled *Tall Story*, the movie version of a successful, if lightweight, Broadway play. But Warner Bros, the production company, were unhappy with two unknowns as the leads and exhanged Beatty for Anthony Perkins, then an idol of the teenage audience at which the film was aimed.

Before beginning filming in September 1959, Jane made her professional stage debut, playing the virginal heroine of *The Moon Is Blue* in a New Jersey local theatre production. To her dismay she found herself floundering. The 'Method' worked well with the kind of emotionally complex characters portrayed by Marlon Brando and James Dean, but it provided little help with the relatively shallow characterisations of light comedy. There were still more readjustments awaiting her in Hollywood.

The first, and easiest, was instant celebrity. As with Henry before her, Jane's first cinema role was a starring one and she received the full blast of the Hollywood publicity machine. She was pictured very much as her father's daughter – a sweet and wholesome all-American girl. The image did not strike her as a particularly accurate one, but she was thankful enough to have kept her understandable nervousness under control and made no attempt to contradict the general view.

The second adjustment was to the art of screen acting. The camera, she quickly discovered, had to be wooed as assiduously as any live audience – and it could be manipulated in just the same way. The final adjustment, and the most immediately painful, involved *Tall Story* itself. It became plain that the film – the story of an ambitious co-ed in pursuit of a campus basketball star – was a fast-moving mix of unexceptional wisecracks and coy sexual humour. When the film was released the following year the critics were universally unimpressed, granting their only plaudits to Jane's performance, though with the inevitable comparisons with her father's talent and some heavy reservations. As *Motion Picture* magazine put it: '(Jane) is unlikely to follow in her father's distinguished footsteps if *Tall Story* is the type of material she will pursue.'

Jane agreed. Lee Strasberg's tuition had prepared her for meatier roles than this but Hollywood in the late fifties had few 'serious' opportunities for an attractive and sexually appealing female newcomer, however talented or well-connected. The American film industry was in a state of uncertainty, beset on one side by television, which offered the main elements of the Hollywood dream more cheaply and conveniently to the consumer, and on the other by profound and accelerating changes in society, which threatened traditional Hollywood even more fundamentally. A rising post-war generation – of which Jane herself was an example – possessed a greater self-awareness than any before and wanted to see that awareness reflected in the cinema. European films were already pointing the way, most notably in the treatment of sexuality. Roger Vadim's hugely successful *And God Created Woman*, made in 1956, showed the commercial possibilities of unrestrained eroticism. Simone Signoret won a Best Actress Academy Award in 1959 for her earthy and honest portrayal of an 'older woman' in the critically acclaimed British film *Room At the Top*, itself a grittily authentic view of a British industrial town. Meanwhile Hollywood still operated under the restraints of the 1934 Production Code which insisted that 'excessive and lustful kissing, lustful embracing, suggestive postures and gestures' were not to be shown.

The American theatre, however, was rather less restrained and, chastened by her first professional experience of Hollywood, Jane returned gratefully to its bosom – to be offered her first Broadway lead, again by Josh Logan who shrewdly planned to open the play at the same time as *Tall Story* was released, thereby doubling the media coverage of his new star. Daniel Taradash's *There Was a Little Girl* seemed to offer Jane everything the cinema had not. It was the melodramatic tale of a young woman raped while en route to a motel tryst with her young lover. Its theme was that a crime can often taint its innocent victim as much as its perpetrator.

Despite the objections of Henry, who regarded the play as exploitative, Jane threw herself into the role. The play opened on 29 February 1960 and ran only sixteen performances. The writing received a critical dismissal, but Jane's performance did not. 'Although Miss Fonda looks a great deal like her father,' wrote Brooks Atkinson of the *New York Times*, 'her acting style is her own.' He went on to praise an 'alert, many-sided performance that is professionally mature'. Other critics agreed, to the extent that she earned the New York Drama Critics' Award for the most promising new actress of the year.

The play was a turning point for Jane, professionally and personally. 'I began to see the problems of Jane Fonda the person were the same as those of Jane Fonda the actress,' she said later. 'Acting, when you're serious about it, is tough. It hurts. It has to hurt, otherwise you're not acting. All you've got to draw upon is yourself. If you're shallow, if you've got no emotional depth, you're not going to act very well, especially in a part that is highly emotional. It will come out all surface and without truth. The serious actor tries to get at the truth of a character. To do that you really have to reach into yourself. I was not used to reaching into myself, and when I did with this part, I was at first surprised to find that there was something there, then astonished to learn how thoroughly well hidden it had been.'

The winter of 1960–1 set the seal on her career. On 29 October she opened in her second Broadway play, Arthur Laurents' *Invitation To a March*. Its theme was the contrast between unpredictable but life-enhancing non-conformity and safe but stultifying convention – a view to which Jane was not unsympathetic, though ironically her role was that of a conventional ingénue with little opportunity for Method technique. Nevertheless the play became her first commercial success, running for three and a half months and gaining her a battery of glowing personal notices. The most eloquent came from Britain's Kenneth Tynan: 'Jane Fonda can quiver like a tuning fork, and her neurotic outbursts are as shocking as the wanton, piecemeal destruction of a priceless harpsichord. What is more, she has extraordinary physical resources.'

The following January she received the accolade she valued most. She auditioned for and was accepted into the Actors Studio proper. Her audition piece was a scene from *Butterfield 8*, John O'Hara's tale of a prostitute trying to go straight, and her director was a small, mannered, somewhat arrogant Greek called Andreas Voutsinas.

Apart from her innate ability, Jane had been prompted to take up acting by a need to gain approval, initially from her father. No approval can be headier or more positive than the enthusiastic applause of audience, but a more personal approbation was just as necessary and, despite his daughter's success, Henry seemed no more capable of giving it than ever. Visiting the set of *Tall Story* he had told a reporter with obvious pride, 'Jane has made more progress in one year than I have in thirty.' He did not, however, tell her.

Jane's first serious relationship, with a young and sensitive fellow member of Strasberg's classes named Timothy Everett, had helped to redress that imbalance. Andreas Voutsinas completed that process and set a pattern for Jane's life that was to continue for many years.

Five years Jane's elder, Voutsinas took Strasberg as his model and had already had a considerable influence as a private acting coach on several young actresses, most notably Anne Bancroft. To many of the Actors Studio crowd he was a self-important and comically obvious manipulator, to others a more sinister Svengali-type figure. Jane's attitude to him was mixed at first, but gradually she came more and more under his spell. Everett provided this analysis of Jane's situation: 'She had this really profound need to get her direction, her sense of herself and of what to do at any given moment, from someone else, and it had to be a man. Now, if what she chose to do turned out to be successful, she would take credit for it herself – she had made the right decision. But if it turned out not to be successful, then she would excuse it by saying that she'd put her trust in someone and he had misguided her – so it was not her fault.'

It was a harsh judgement but it contained a strong grain of truth. Everett's view of Voutsinas, the man who eventually replaced him in Jane's affections, was no less telling: 'I think Jane's main fascination with Andreas had to do with the fact that he brought out the meanness of her personality. He showed her a completely different side of herself. She was sick of being the goody-goody girl – it nauseated her that people only saw her in one way. Andreas was showing her – or she thought he was – how to express all the hidden rage she had, how to be mean and ugly without feeling guilty about it. She liked what that did for her. Once she learned to handle it as though it were a natural part of herself, instead of some kind of abnormality to be kept buried, it gave her a sense of power and confidence she'd never had before.'

For all his faults – and his manner ensured that other people would always be keen to point them out – Voutsinas set in motion the first of a series of self-liberations that would become one of the most important aspects of Jane's career. Later she would cite two major influences on her life at this time: the first was psycho-analysis, which she had been undergoing in accordance with Actors Studio practice; the second was Andreas.

Voutsinas went with her as a private acting coach on her second Hollywood excursion in April 1961. Despite her previous misgivings about the film industry, and the fact that her part was a relatively minor one, Jane regarded her second film as an opportunity to redress the girl-next-door image of *Tall Story*. It could not have been more different. *Walk On the Wild Side* was based on Nelson Algren's realistic novel of New Orleans' seamier side. It told the story of a penniless farmer (an unlikely Laurence Harvey) tracing a former lover to a brothel where she is the favourite of the lesbian madame. Jane played Kitty Twist, a petulant and amoral thief who winds up in the same brothel. It was, Jane enthused, 'a wonderful acting part. She's like a cat, ends up ratting on everybody and getting everybody killed. I never would have thought anyone would offer me this kind of part. I've always been wanted for the ingénue, the girl next door . . . People will remember Kitty Twist.'

That hope proved illusory. Cited as an 'adult' entertainment, the film diluted the grimy and poignant realism of the novel into a lurid and cliché-ridden melodrama. Only the prowling alley cat in Saul Bass's stunning title sequence and Elmer Bernstein's pounding score escaped a critical slamming.

Undeterred, Jane went straight into another film with similar pretensions. *The Chapman Report* was the film version of an Irving Wallace bestseller about a Kinsey-style team of researchers investigating the sexual habits of women in the Los Angeles area. The subject matter was considered sensational by the standards of 1961, but once more Hollywood flirted with the idea of sexual liberation rather than dealing honestly with the substance. The result was a glossy soap opera, promising a great deal more than it was ever prepared to give.

Jane auditioned for the role of a nymphomaniac housewife and, rather to her surprise, found herself cast as a frigid young middle-class widow – a woman eager for love, but terrified by sex and hiding the conflict behind a

82

polite mask. Jane knew the character's background well and had no difficulty in expressing her inner tension, but the film was poorly received.

Not all Jane's image-building, however, was conducted on screen. She was becoming a favourite with the press with an outspokenness her father would never have dreamed of. She allegedly shocked the hardened Hollywood gossip columnist Hedda Hopper by declaring marriage obsolete. She was photographed semi-nude for *Cavalier* magazine. There were reports of difficulties with directors (mainly the result of Voutsinas' on-set advice) and suggestions of a refusal to wear underwear in scenes when ordered to do so. When she tried to buy herself out of her initial contract with Josh Logan, only to find that his friendship with Henry did not blunt his business sense, she blasted him in print. This upset Henry, but not as much as his daughter's increasingly personal comments on him.

'I know it's very strange that a girl should feel competitive against her father,' she said, 'but that's the way I feel. I always feel that I have to prove to him that I'm right. Somehow he can't seem to separate my being a daughter from my being an actress . . . Before I went to analysis, I told everyone lies . . . I learned that I had grown up in an atmosphere where nobody told the truth. Everyone was so concerned with appearances that life was just one big lie. Now all I want to do is live a life of truth.'

Henry endured the onslaught stoically. He had no way of knowing that a lot worse was to follow.

Henry Fonda

HENRY'S CONCERN over Jane's well-publicised career had its counterpart in a nagging but no less comfortable anxiety about his own. He was nearing his mid-fifties now and, despite his enduring looks, he was aware that advancing years were rarely kind to leading men. Of the stars he had known from his early days in Hollywood only James Stewart and John Wayne seemed to be in regular employment.

Time, however, would prove Henry's worries to be ill-founded. His image as an actor had never depended on youthful vigour or straightforward handsomeness. Even as a young actor there had been something patriarchal in his manner; age merely transformed youthful idealism into a measured but equally high principled maturity. Likewise the sparky anger of a Tom Joad changed easily into the more crotchety displeasure of an older man.

By 1959 he had been a star for twenty-five years – and another twenty-one years of stage and screen success lay ahead of him. Only towards the very end of that time would he match his earlier triumphs – in terms of both popular and critical success – but the performances he was to give would only rarely dip below his own exacting standards.

After his run of four successive stage hits between 1948 and 1958, he established a pattern of alternating between Broadway and Hollywood, with occasional forays into television, but Broadway almost always had precedence. Several of the screen performances he gave were undertaken with thinly disguised reluctance, chiefly for the purposes of necessary cash. This was certainly the case in his first television series, *The Deputy*, which he began filming in 1959. It was not a success. Henry was featured as Simon Fry, chief marshal of Arizona Territory in the 1880s with Allen Case as his assistant, the deputy of the title. Part of the problem was that the series was *The Deputy* vaunted as an 'adult' Western but tight scheduling left little opportunity for quality work. The main difficulty, however, was that Henry only starred in six of the the thirty-nine half-hour episodes. For the majority he would appear in the initial scene-setting and then bow out, leaving the bulk of the action to Allen Case. Understandably audiences who had switched on to see Henry Fonda were not impressed.

In the autumn of 1959 Henry hurried back to New York to begin rehearsals for a new play, *Silent Night, Lonely Night* by Robert Anderson. He starred with Barbara Bel Geddes in a tale of two lonely people finding each other one Christmas Eve in a New England inn. The play opened in December and the critical acclaim went to the actors' performances rather than the playwright's efforts, but the production was a commercial success.

The next year saw a repetition of the same pattern: a summer spent on his second, and final, season of *The Deputy*, followed by a play – a slight comedy called *Critic's Choice*, about a Broadway drama critic embarrassed by having to review a very bad play written by his wife.

In 1961 three films filled the space vacated by television. Two of Fonda's roles were cameos, the first a grizzled buffalo hunter, heavily disguised by flowing locks and a gigantic moustache, in *How the West Was Won*; on occasion visually spectacular, it was an otherwise undistinguished exercise in the wide-screen, three-camera format of Cinerama – later replaced by 70-millimetre. Henry went on to portray General Theodore Roosevelt Jr in Darryl F Zanuck's documentary-style recreation of D-Day, *The Longest Day*. More substantial was the role of a controversial candidate for secretary of state in *Advise and Consent*, the film version of Allen Drury's monumental political bestseller. This was the first in a trio of films with a political background, each successive part offering the actor further 'promotion' until, in *Fail Safe* in 1964, he reached the apotheosis of the presidency itself.

Towards the end of the year he was in New York for *A Gift of Time* with Olivia De Havilland. Written by Garson Kanin, it was a harrowing and factual account of a novelist dying of cancer who, with his wife's connivance, curtailed his final agony by cutting his wrists. Fonda passionately believed in the play and fought to do it, against the advice of his agents who regarded the story as too depressing. They were proved right. When the play opened on 22 February 1962 the first night audience heard it out in a hushed silence. It closed shortly afterwards – Henry's first flop in fourteen years on Broadway. The failure set an unfortunate tone for the year. As 'penance' Henry agreed to do *Spencer's Mountain* – a script which he claimed was 'old-fashioned corn – it will set movies back twenty-five years'. Despite forming the basis of *The Waltons* television series a decade later, the film earned a critical dismissal as 'a package of piety and prurience' from Judith Crist of the *New York Herald Tribune*. Most of her fellow critics agreed, but the film's commercial success helped

to restore Henry's financial fortunes. His professional self-esteem, however, suffered a further blow when he learned that, without consulting him, his agents had turned down Edward Albee's spectacularly successful stage play *Who's Afraid of Virginia Woolf?* As soon as filming on *Spencer's Mountain* was finished he hurried back to Broadway to see the play. 'I sat there sliding farther and farther down in my seat,' he said. 'I think I would have given up any role I've ever played – Tom Joad or Mister Roberts, any of them – to have had a chance at that part. And I couldn't even say, "This should have been my part", because up on that stage Arthur Hill was giving an absolutely perfect performance.' The knowledge that Albee had personally regarded Henry as ideal for the role did nothing to improve matters.

There were fluctuating fortunes in Henry's private life, too, at the

87

beginning of the sixties, quite apart from Jane's public criticisms. The decade began with a shock. On 1 January 1960 Henry's first wife, Margaret Sullavan was found dying from a sleeping pill overdose at a hotel in New Haven, Connecticut. The lively and tempestuous woman Henry had known had become increasingly moody and depressed over the years, largely as a result of worsening deafness. She had been starring in a pre-Broadway try-out of a new play, entitled – with a grim irony for Henry – *Sweet Love Remembered*. But she had been having difficulties with the role, and worry had led to sleeplessness. Nine months later, Margaret's daughter Bridget, with whom Jane and Peter had grown up, also took an overdose – at the age of twenty-one. She had been suffering from nervous disorders for years, to be finally diagnosed as an epileptic. Once more the spectre of suicide hovered about the Fondas.

Early in 1961 Henry said goodbye in a less final, but no less painful manner, to his fourth wife. The unending social whirl which had been his marriage to Afdera had lasted longer than most of their friends and families had expected. As with Susan Blanchard, Henry had no wish to seek yet another divorce, however unhappy the immediate situation, but Afdera's affair with an Englishman brought their problems sharply into focus. At the divorce hearing in Mexico Afdera insisted that she was to blame: 'I was too young,' she said. 'I was too headstrong. I was immature.' Later she amplified her feelings in terms that had strong echoes of Susan Blanchard's words some five years earlier: '(Fonda) is a strange man in the sense that he has this block and you can't reach him any more. He has his whole private world. He could have been a monk. If I had married him ten years later, I would have been a good wife to him, and understood him and never let him go. He could have been a friend, he could have been a father. Certainly he was a lover. Everything. I didn't give him a chance.'

Once the divorce was over, Henry vowed never to marry again. He regarded himself as a 'staid mid-Westerner', not the kind of fickle Lothario his marital record suggested. But the idea of marriage – for all his silences, for all his inability to tolerate open displays of emotion or strong feeling – was deeply ingrained in him. Within two years he had met the woman who would become his fifth, and last wife.

Her name was Shirlee Mae Adams. Tall, attractive and outgoing, she was an airline hostess and part-time model, in her mid-twenties when she first met the fifty-seven-year-old actor. Unlike her two immediate predecessors, Henry's celebrity did not prompt the initial interest. Despite gaining her first glimpse of the actor at the premiere of *The Longest Day* she was not a movie-goer and the Fonda name rang no particular bells. Like Henry, however, she came from the mid-West and shared many of his values. Her liveliness was matched by a commonsensical, down-to-earth quality which all Henry's previous marital escapades had lacked. It became clear soon

The Longest Day

88

after their first date – engineered unwittingly by a Hollywood press agent who had asked Shirlee along to a dinner with Henry simply because the PR man knew her to be a good talker – that here was the stability Fonda needed. They began seeing each other regularly, but Henry made it obvious that marriage was out of the question, as was a 'live-in' relationship, which Fonda's sense of propriety could not allow. To his mind, the fact that Shirlee went home at the end of every evening satisfied his conscience. That this attitude implied more than a degree of self-deception did not escape the attention of his children, particularly Peter. 'His duplicity,' he said, 'blew our minds.'

Since entering the University of Nebraska, Peter had given the impression of settling down, at least in comparison with the neurotic outbursts of his adolescence. Outwardly he conformed, inwardly his ambitions concentrated on the family business. The first fruit of this decision was a leading role in a college production of the comedy *Harvey*. During rehearsals for *Silent Night, Lonely Night* in 1959, Henry flew to Omaha to see the play. 'Here were these college kids, eighteen to twenty-two, playing people in their fifties,' he recalled. 'They were playing the parts as though they were ninety-nine. The lawyer, supposedly in his late forties, came creeping in on a cane. My boy Peter was smart. He played it straight and landed every single laugh. By God, his name isn't Fonda for nothing!'

This was one occasion when Henry appeared to have no difficulty in communicating his enthusiasm to his offspring. Encouraged by his father's obvious delight, Peter decided to abandon his academic studies and take up a professional acting career. The following year he joined a summer stock company in Fishkill in New York State. That autumn he auditioned for his first Broadway role in a comedy called *Blood, Sweat and Stanley Poole* by James and William Goldman. Initially he was turned down but after a six-month pause the producers invited him to audition a second time and he was awarded the part.

The play opened on 5 October 1961. It was a lightweight tale on a military theme, set in World War Two, and its run only lasted two months. But Peter's personal reviews were good. 'This is no doubt the very last morning in which Peter Fonda will have to be identified as Henry Fonda's son,' wrote Walter Kerr in the *New York Herald Tribune*. Psychologically the play was an enormous boost to the young actor's sensitive but by no means diminutive ego. 'Now I can stand on my own two feet,' he announced, 'and dispense with anybody who comes up to me and says, "You are here because of who you are and not because of your talent."' As if to underline this, he married twenty-one-year-old Susan Brewer, a student and stepdaughter of Howard Hughes' right hand man, three days after the opening.

When the play closed he and the new Mrs Fonda (at the time the only female member of the Fonda clan bearing that title) flew to Hollywood for Peter to audition for the lead in *PT 109*, the story of President Kennedy's wartime exploits. Instead he won the male lead in a sickly-sweet romance entitled *Tammy and the Doctor* aimed at much the same audience as that of Jane's *Tall Story*.

The Tammy of the title was a young backwoods girl prone to homespun philosophising and neatly solving the unremarkable problems of friends and acquaintances, a kind of older and sexier Pollyanna. This was the third *Tammy* film and the second starring Sandra Dee, a young actress specialising in glamorous teenagers teetering on the edge of (married) sexual awakening. As the beau urging her towards matrimony, Peter was required to be little more than charming and generally eligible. Privately he

Tammy and the Doctor,
with Sandra Dee

re-named the film 'Tammy and the Schmuckface', a view largely endorsed, through in politer terms, by the few reviewers who commented on it.

Peter's lifestyle at this time was almost aggressively conformist. With his short hair, neat suits, fashionable Beverly Hills home – with a Jaguar and then a gull wing Mercedes parked in front – he saw himself as 'the ultimate David Eisenhower'. He told *Playboy* some years later: 'I was thinking about flying around in 320 Cessnas, travelling the world over like I was James Bond. Always trying to create an elegant, conservative, graceful fashion thing. Trying to emulate my father, whom I saw as an elegant, graceful, conservative man.'

His first film roles mirrored the 'straight' image – and were correspondingly unremarkable. In Carl Foreman's sprawling, anti-war World War Two epic *The Victors* he played a small role as an enthusiastic newcomer to an army squad. In *The Young Lovers* he was back in the lead as a college student whose girlfriend becomes pregnant and refuses an abortion, effectively ending their affair. Most notable of these early performances, and the one which engaged Peter most fully, was the part of a suicidal mental patient in director Robert Rossen's last film, *Lilith*.

Left: Tammy and the Doctor
Below: The Victors
Overleaf: The Young Lovers

93

Starring Warren Beatty and Jean Seberg, it was a poetic and sensitive study of madness, but its qualities were not immediately appreciated by either critics or public, and Peter's contribution was heavily depleted at the editing stage.

His conventional image may or may not have impressed Henry, but it appealed to Jane even less than it did to the movie-going public. Having moved from the Bohemianism of the Actors Studio to a more sensational form of self-liberation as a growing sex symbol, she looked with horror on her younger brother's conservative materialism. Soon she was as alienated from him as she had become from their father.

But Peter's desire to conform was as much a form of personal experimentation as Jane's need to be 'the rattiest, wannest, most straggle-haired' member of Lee Strasberg's acting classes. He might belong to the Republican party and buy his wife fur coats, but he also felt the need to keep private demons of self-doubt and self-loathing at bay with regular applications of wine, whisky, vodka and finally marijuana. He had been introduced to the illicit weed by a fellow cast member during the filming of *The Victors*. He quickly discovered that it was 'a way to get past some of the daily abrasion of living that can hang you up.'

Peter was now on the point of a change of lifestyle even more spectacular than that attempted by Jane. America's idealism of the early sixties, largely fostered by the Kennedy presidency, was moving on into a more hedonistic, anti-materialist phase: the world of Flower Power and hippy communes, 'dropping out' of a society whose main achievements seemed to be gross commercialism or the violence of the escalating war in Vietnam, and 'tuning in' to a private mental landscape, with the help of mind-expanding drugs like LSD, mescalin and other hallucinogens. By the mid-sixties Hollywood gave the impression of being dominated by the anthem-makers of the rising youth culture, the pop music industry; long hair was suddenly fashionable, as was experimentation with drugs.

Peter's first experience of the then still legal LSD came in the autumn of 1965. It took place in the Mohave desert where he had driven with two friends. 'As that first trip progressed,' he said later, 'I thought about my father and about my relationship with him and my mother and my sister. And suddenly I busted through the whole thing and related everything. There was no more worry about my father, mother and sister. I began to feel really on top of all my problems. I had no further relationship with the past; I'd kicked it.'

Ten more trips followed in swift succession, completing a process of self-revelation. In a few short weeks Peter had come to terms with problems that would continue to plague Jane for years to come. The change was as much outward as inward. To Henry's bewilderment, his son turned virtually overnight from an arch-conformist to an arch-rebel, sporting long

The Young Lovers

hair and tinted glasses and expounding the virtues of psychedelic drugs to anyone who would listen.

The effects of this transformation were not confined to Peter's private life. Since *The Young Lovers* was released in 1964 his acting career had been in the doldrums. Now he attracted the attention of a small, independent production company called American International Pictures, noted for its low-budget exploitation films aimed mainly at teenage and drive-in audiences. Its leading light was producer-director Roger Corman. Corman was something of a Hollywood anomaly, combining intellectual pretensions, largely displayed in a respected series of Edgar Allen Poe adaptations in the early sixties, with the reputation of being the film capital's most prolific creator of low-budget 'quickies'; some of his early movies – whose titles included *Attack of the Crab Monsters* and *Teenage Caveman* – had been filmed in under three days.

Corman was keen to make a film exploiting the notoriety of California's Hell's Angel motorcycling gangs and as the openly rebellious son of a totem

Below: *Lilith*, with Jean Seberg and Warren Beatty
Overleaf: *The Wild Angels*

figure of the older generation, Peter Fonda seemed ideal for the lead. The result was *The Wild Angels*, released in 1966. It consisted of a freewheeling succession of drunken orgies, motorcycle derbies and gang fights – the climax taking place at the church funeral of a gang member where a preacher is beaten up and the girlfriend of the deceased raped behind her ex-boyfriend's swastika-draped coffin. Calculated to tread heavily on the sensibilities of anyone over twenty-five, it succeeded brilliantly and became an enormous commercial success.

As gangleader Heavenly Blues, Peter, with his lean, angular frame and fine features, seemed an unlikely tough guy and the youthful creed he voiced vague in the extreme ('We want to be free to do what we want to do . . . we want to be free to ride without being hassled by the man . . . we want to get loaded . . . we want to have a good time.'). But there was a conviction in what he said and a laid-back yet patrician authority in his manner that appealed to young audiences.

The film's success turned him into one of the first cinema stars of the new youth culture; posters featuring Peter Fonda astride the motorcycle he had ridden in the film sold in huge quantities. *The Wild Angels* might have been a far remove from the supreme artistry of *The Grapes of Wrath* – and Peter's performance competent rather than classic – but the film did enable him to achieve the kind of radical heroism Henry had achieved with Tom Joad a generation before. In increasingly radical times it was an important step forward.

DESPITE HER avowed desire to 'live a life of truth' Jane's success in doing so in her acting career was still relatively limited. She was an attractive and promising young actress, capable of transmitting sultriness and innocence in roughly equal amounts – a mixture which served her well for the stock of Hollywood ingénue roles of the day – but underlying this was a deep strain of neurotic energy which could not be so easily harnessed. It manifested itself in her staccato style of speech, the swift yet graceful manner in which she moved, suggesting both purposefulness and restlessness.

One outlet for this combination of characteristics had been provided by her cinematic debut in *Tall Story*, and that was comedy. Early in 1962 the opportunity arose again – with a role in *Period of Adjustment*, the film version of an unusually conventional Tennessee Williams' play, which detailed two twenty-four-hour crises in contrasting marriages – one just begun and the other on the point of break-up. In a screenplay that, for all the banality of the plot, was wittier, sharper written and had considerably more depth of characterisation than anything she had tackled before, Jane felt herself blossom.

'It was an enormous challenge for me,' she said later, 'especially because with my two previous films I felt I had tried but not gotten a good grasp on the characters I was playing. With *Adjustment* I felt that I finally got hold of a character and . . . well, I liked what I did.'

The critics agreed with her. 'Jane Fonda plays a nervous Southern bride, anxious in more than one sense,' wrote Stanley Kaufman in the *New Republic*. 'Her comic touch is as sure as her serious one. Besides the gift of timing, she has what lies below all comedy: confidence in one's perception of the humorous – where it begins and especially where it ends.' Her success persuaded her that films rather than the stage were the proper home for her talents. 'Somehow making movies gets to you,' she said. 'It's ego-battering – you're up one day and down the next – and it's much tougher work for an actor, because with all the various things involved it's harder to create a performance. When I did *Adjustment*, I finally began to feel like an experienced film actress, and I decided movies were for me.'

This happy decision was put immediately to the test with her next film. Called *In the Cool of the Day*, it featured Jane as a spoilt and tubercular New York businessman's wife enjoying a last fling with a middle-aged and married Englishman, played by Peter Finch, among the ruins of ancient Greece. It was an uneasy mixture of travelogue and distinctly uninspired soap opera and it did little for the careers of any of the participants.

There was a more public disappointment awaiting Jane on her return from filming in Greece. Earlier in 1962 she had agreed to do another Broadway play, a comedy entitled *The Fun Couple*, on condition that

Below and right: *Period of Adjustment*

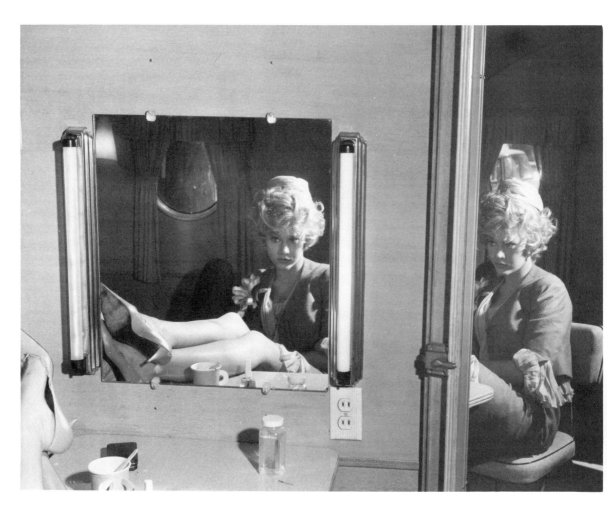

Andreas Voutsinas directed it. Voutsinas was keen to make his mark as a director and Jane wanted to both repay his help and to vindicate her faith in him. Unfortunately the play, which had been written by two novice dramatists, was badly flawed and Voutsinas' direction was both vague and off-key. Long before the New York opening it was obvious that something was seriously wrong, but the growing air of desperation only seemed to strengthen Jane's championship of Andreas. It was a trait that, however admirable, would cause her embarrassment later in her career: her loyalty, once given, was total.

The play opened on Broadway on 26 October and was an immediate and humiliating flop; there were only three performances. Its failure reinforced Jane's decision to seek a career in films, and she would make only one more stage appearance, in an Actors Studio production of Eugene O'Neill's *Strange Interlude* in the spring of 1963.

Below: Jane on the rooftop of London's Savoy Hotel during the filming of *In the Cool of the Day*
Right: *In the Cool of the Day*, with Peter Finch

Jane went from that into another film version of a successful Broadway comedy, *Sunday in New York*, which told the story of a young woman's amatory and farcical adventures in New York. Since it was a typical Hollywood product of its time, sex was treated largely by innuendo, the heroine was resolutely virginal – and always rescued by a protective brother when she showed signs of becoming otherwise – and marriage was signalled as the right end for all the leading characters. But Jane enjoyed making it and surmised, quite rightly, that it would boost her career as an attractive and reliable comedienne. As it happened it was her attractiveness, or sexiness, rather than her comic talent that would determine the next development in her career – and not in Hollywood, but Europe.

The French cinema had been experiencing a renaissance toward the end of the fifties, posing an increasing threat to Hollywood's export markets with its fresher and less inhibited approach to film-making. Roger Vadim had first broken into the world market with *And God Created Woman*, making an international star of his then wife Brigitte Bardot. His vanguard action had soon been consolidated by a group of critics-turned-filmmakers, known collectively as the New Wave. Ironically their desire to make films had been prompted by a deep admiration of the products of Hollywood, including the works of directors like Samuel Fuller and Don Siegel, who had received scant acclaim in their home country.

Realistic as always, however, Hollywood now began to respond to the challenge by joining rather than trying to beat its rival. MGM was one of a number of major production companies investing in European films and in 1963 it decided to back a thriller, heavily laced with sex and violence, called *Les Félins* or *Joy House*.

On the face of it it seemed a good investment. The film was to be directed by a respected French director, René Clement; Alain Delon, a leading French heart-throb, would guarantee local interest, while two imported American actresses would boost the international appeal. One was Lola Albright, the other Jane Fonda. Jane accepted the role out of a strong desire to see the new French cinema at work. Its aims and methods, with its hand-held camerawork, improvised dialogue and sexual frankness, seemed to break out of the Hollywood straitjacket which she had resented increasingly from *Tall Story* onward; here, apparently, was a truth which could not be found in American films.

In the event *Joy House* had many of the trappings of the New Wave – black and white photography, a semi-improvised script and a great deal of complicated bed-hopping – but little of the substance. Its rambling and implausible plot involved a gangster on the run (Delon) who finds refuge in a Gothic château where Albright and Fonda vie for his attentions. Somewhere in the background lurks Albright's existing lover, who also happens to be a gangster on the run. The silliness of the story was matched

Sunday in New York, with Cliff Robertson

by the quality of the dialogue, which was filmed in French.

The film did moderate business in France and was slammed in America, but Jane was far from disappointed. At a stroke she had broken out of the old Hollywood mould, carving a place for herself in the new, hedonistic, free-thinking 'swinging sixties', much as her brother Peter was to do two years later. She had also become a French media star.

Launched on a wave of MGM publicity, she won instant celebrity, delighting the French with her fractured use of their language – revived from her Parisian excursion five years before – and engaging in a brief flirtation with co-star Delon, which fully occupied the gossip columns. She was interviewed on television; her face was splashed across newspapers and magazines; there was even a pop song in her honour. Eventually she earned the ultimate Gallic accolade as 'the American Brigitte Bardot'.

Such an image was bound to attract the interest of the man who had established the fame and the notoriety of the original BB. Since Bardot had become a star, Roger Vadim had been divorced and moved on to create two more stars in the same blonde, pouting, sex-kittenish mould, Annette Stroyberg and Catherine Deneuve, each of whom had borne him a child, though he had only married Stroyberg for a brief time. In 1963 he was in his mid-thirties, a man with an avowed contempt for conventional sexual morality and, as a result, a formidable sexual reputation. He had also just broken up with Catherine Deneuve and was looking for a young actress to give international appeal to a projected re-make of a classic French film of the early fifties, *La Ronde*. 'La BB Americaine' seemed ideal.

Despite her nickname, Jane approached Vadim with a great deal of trepidation. Underneath her newly acquired image, there were still powerful traces of the well-brought-up, upper middle-class American young woman. She was pleasantly surprised. In place of a rampant satyr she found a quiet, civilised, intelligent man with a somewhat professorial manner, inwardly self-assured but outwardly almost shy. 'I was absolutely floored,' she said later. 'He was the antithesis of what I'd been told . . . I discovered a very gentle man. So many men in America are . . . men-men, always having to prove their strength and masculinity. Vadim was not afraid to be vulnerable – even feminine, in a way. And I was terrified of being vulnerable.' Their affair began during the filming of *La Ronde*, where most of Jane's performance seemed to take place in bed, sometimes with a suggestion of nudity – an aspect she found so traumatic that she went to great pains to inform the French press that she had been wearing bra and panties throughout. By the time the film was finished she and Vadim were living together.

The relationship was to last six years. In many ways it was ideal for Jane at that time. Vadim combined the solidity and authority she admired in her father with the sensitivity and responsiveness she had found in Timothy

Everett and Andreas Voutsinas, who had returned to America during the Delon flirtation. Like Voutsinas Vadim was another Svengali figure and just as likely to exploit Jane for his own career ends, but he also propounded and lived a hedonistic and sexually permissive philosophy that Jane then regarded as a necessary, if occasionally uncomfortable, part of her self-liberation. It was not long before she was propounding the same philosophy, and attempting to act it out, chiefly in the films she made for the French director.

The result was a curious dichotomy in her career. In France Jane became known as Vadim's new protegée, one of the premier stars of the new permissiveness: she appeared topless and discreetly nude for him in *The Game is Over*, a sumptuous and highly charged version of Emile Zola's *La Curée*; one of the director's most acclaimed successes – at least in Europe – it gave Jane the opportunity to portray a woman in love with an honesty and a completeness she would never have been allowed in Hollywood. In *Metzengerstein*, the first episode of a portmanteau film called *Spirits of the Dead* and based on stories by Edgar Allan Poe, Jane wore revealing medieval costume, participated in an orgy and toyed with suggestions of incest – which she later hotly denied as intentional – when her phantom lover was played by her brother Peter. And in *Barbarella*, one of Vadim's

Previous page: *Circle of Love*
Left: *Barbarella*
Right: *Sunday in New York*

110

greatest commercial successes, he set out to picture her as 'the ultimate sex symbol . . . a kind of sexual Alice in Wonderland of the future', where Jane played a scantily clad innocent abroad in a bizarrely erotic 40th century. A glossy fantasy, it was intended to debunk conventional sexual morality but succeeded largely in wallowing in the uninhibited alternative.

In America, on the other hand, Jane was climbing to stardom as a vibrant, sexy but entirely wholesome comedienne. She appeared as such in *Cat Ballou*, the biggest commercial success of her career so far, which she made in California between *La Ronde* and *The Game is Over*. It was an inspired spoof Western, as liberating in its debunking view of Hollywood's Wild West as anything Vadim attempted in relation to sex. Jane played a former schoolteacher who recruits a gang of wholly unlikely outlaws in order to avenge the death of her rancher father. The film won an Oscar for Lee Marvin in a dual role as a tin-nosed villain and drunkenly inept former gunfighter, turning him instantly from a reliable Hollywood 'heavy' into a major star. But it was the conviction and credibility of Jane's central performance that provided a solid, dramatic anchorage for the wilder goings-on around her. She displayed a similar awareness of the basis of comedy in *Any Wednesday*, which detailed the trials and tribulations of a mistress turning thirty and debating whether to find marital happiness with her businessman lover's colleague or continue as she is.

More successful was her appearance in the film version of the Neil Simon Broadway hit, *Barefoot in the Park*, in which she played a boisterous and unconventional free spirit newly married to a staid and shockable Robert Redford. It was one of the major box office successes of 1967.

Not all of Jane's Hollywood movies during her Vadim period were comedies, however. The more seriously dramatic work she was doing in Europe led to two roles in *The Chase* and *Hurry Sundown*. Ironically it was not the French films themselves that prompted the offers – since all but *Barbarella* did poorly in the States; rather it was the publicity that arose out of them. Early in 1965, shortly after the completion of *Cat Ballou*, *La Ronde*, now re-titled *Circle of Love* in the English language version, was advertised on Broadway by a seventy-foot high billboard displaying a gigantic, bare-bottomed nude likeness of Jane. Outraged she promptly threatened to sue, which only added to the general interest. But the uproar drew Jane to the attention of producer Sam Spiegel who was then casting *The Chase*. After seeing her in the still unreleased *Cat Ballou* he hired her.

Jane's role, however, as the sluttish wife of an escaped convict returning to a corrupt Texan town was not markedly different in kind from her Kitty Twist characterisation in *Walk On the Wild Side*. Intended as an allegory of the current American scene, the film emerged as a pretentious and overblown melodrama which even Marlon Brando's presence, as the town's sheriff and single worthy personage, was unable to save. However Jane's

Previous page and left:
Cat Ballou
Right: *Any Wednesday*

Southern drawl, and her European permissive image, impressed director-producer Otto Preminger who cast her in *Hurry Sundown*. Like *The Chase*, the film started with lofty intentions: it was a tale of racial conflict in the Deep South between degenerate ruling whites and oppressed and decent blacks. But the end result was a steamy, cliché-ridden saga which so overloaded the negro Civil Rights argument as to make itself ludicrous. Jane played the discontented and oversexed wife of the leading white villain (Michael Caine), and the only aspect of her performance to

gain universal attention was a scene in which she was required to fondle a saxophone played by her screen husband while kneeling between his legs. Even Vadim might have balked at so blatant a form of sexual symbolism. Neither *Hurry Sundown* nor *The Chase* were notable successes, critically or commercially.

Henry had initially viewed Jane's liaison with Vadim with much the same distaste that he had displayed toward Andreas Voutsinas, whom he had regarded as a parasite. When Jane was in America in 1965 to film *The Chase*, she and Vadim, much to Henry's embarrassment, moved into Malibu, only a short distance from Henry's California home. He paid them a visit soon afterwards, fully prepared to walk in on a fullblown orgy, and to his surprise entered a quiet domestic scene. Like his daughter before him, Henry found Vadim to be a friendly and civilised man, with whom he had a surprising amount in common, including a passion for fishing.

It was largely through Vadim's agency that Jane began to allow the very real affection she felt for her father to surface again through the layers of resentment with which she had publicly battered him. Henry, too, was in a

Previous page: With Marlon Brando during the filming of *The Chase*
Left: *The Chase*
Right: *Barefoot in the Park*

119

mood to be more forgiving – mainly due to the influence of the patient, uncomplicated nature of Shirlee Mae Adams. He could not, however, approve of Jane and Vadim's 'live-in' relationship. On 15 August 1965 the couple corrected even that by flying to Las Vegas and getting married – though in a characteristically unconventional manner. A violin orchestra of female musicians in skin-tight, blue sequinned gowns played the wedding music, Vadim forgot the ring and after the ceremony the wedding party sat down to watch a striptease enactment of the French Revolution which featured a naked showgirl enduring a mock-guillotining to the strains of Ravel's *Bolero*. It could all have been a sequence from a Vadim film.

Perhaps Jane's belated legitimisation of her relationship pricked Henry's conscience or simply helped to renew his faith in marriage, for on 3 December – shortly after opening in his first Broadway play since the failure of *A Gift of Time* – he too took the plunge in a simple ceremony on Long Island. 'After stepping up to bat five times,' he commented later, 'I finally hit a home run.'

THE PLAY in which Henry had opened in the autumn of 1965 was entitled *Generation*. It was a lightweight comedy about the reaction of a conservative businessman to his daughter's marriage to an anti-establishment drop-out. The irony of the theme was not lost on Henry. 'I played a confused father,' he said later. 'I was a living authority on the subject.'

Films had kept him fully occupied during his absence from the theatre and he had played a wide variety of roles, from two military cameos – as an admiral in Otto Preminger's ponderous World War Two drama *In Harm's Way* and as an intelligence officer in *The Battle of the Bulge* – to a presidential candidate in *The Best Man* and an elected president narrowly averting nuclear war in *Fail Safe*. There had been two Westerns with a comic slant: the underrated *The Rounders* with Glenn Ford and a re-make of a quirky television play set in a gambling saloon, *A Big Hand for the Little Lady*. The most embarrassing exercise of the period was a part in a coy sex comedy called *Sex and the Single Girl*, which borrowed its title but nothing else from Helen Gurley Brown's bestseller. Clearly Henry was not tempted to follow the path Jane was then blazing in Europe, despite a brief excursion into European cinema when he appeared in a French-Italian-West German co-produced portmanteau film on an espionage theme, *The Dirty Game*.

In August 1966 he was in California filming an off-beat, anti-heroic Western called *Welcome to Hard Times* when the movie's title suddenly took on a wider and ominous meaning. Peter, whose *The Wild Angels* had opened earlier that year, was arrested for possession of narcotics.

Henry's reconciliation with his children had continued apace over the previous year; he was now beginning to admit publicly that he might not have been a particularly good father and that he might have had something to do with the alienation of his offspring. But Peter still remained a distant

Left: *The Battle of the Bulge*
Overleaf, left: *The Rounders*
Overleaf, right: *Sex and the Single Girl*

123

figure. LSD might have helped him to come to terms with his feelings for his father, but Henry's blanket disapproval of drug-taking kept the barriers fully intact. Peter was all the more surprised then when Henry appeared in court on his behalf, announcing 'I am here to give moral or any other support to my son.' Jane too pledged unequivocal support, publicly declaring her brother's innocence and offering financial backing for the trial – no mean gesture in itself since she was in the process of suing *Playboy* magazine for publishing unauthorised nude photographs of herself taken on the set of *The Game is Over*. Despite Peter's avowed interest in drug-taking, the evidence against him was uncertain and the jury were unable to reach a unanimous verdict.

The case re-established a family closeness that had not existed since their earliest time in Hollywood. Plenty of problems remained but the days of public sniping were over. It was a relief to them all. The incident, however, did not – as Henry had hoped – deflect Peter from his drug-centred, Flower Power lifestyle and in 1967 he was busily involved in *The Trip*, the

first Hollywood film to attempt to reproduce a hallucinogenic drug experience on screen. Like *The Wild Angels*, it was made for American International by Roger Corman, though sections were directed in Corman's absence by Peter and his friend Dennis Hopper, a young character actor who had married Peter's childhood friend, Brooke Hayward. Hopper, then in his early thirties, had a reputation for being 'difficult' on set and in fact he and Fonda quarrelled bitterly during the making of *The Trip*. Yet both were agreed on the necessity of making films out of the Hollywood mould – not unsurprisingly the kind of low-budget, youth-orientated movies at which Roger Corman excelled. 'There's a better chance of honesty in a $400,000 picture than there is in a two million dollar picture,' Peter told the

Below: *The Trip*
Right: *Easy Rider*

cinema trade press later that year. The following year, with *Easy Rider*, he would provide a spectacular justification of that remark.

The script for *The Trip* was written by another friend, a 'B' film actor of almost ten years' standing whose name was Jack Nicholson. The next year would also launch Nicholson as a major star, but his work on *The Trip* was not one of his successes.

The story featured Peter as a disillusioned advertising executive seeking enlightenment through his first experience of LSD. The bulk of the film described that experience with a kaleidoscopic array of technical effects and touches borrowed from directors like Bergman and Fellini. Peter had great hopes for the film, not least because of the amount of nudity displayed by himself and his co-star Susan Strasberg. But even that failed to arouse much public or critical interest. Not only did the film seem to lack coherence but the young audience at which it was specifically aimed did not recognise it as a particularly accurate reflection of the LSD experience. That had to wait for the following year and the Beatles' cartoon film *The Yellow Submarine*, which drew heavily on the visual effects of drug-heightened awareness, though its makers denied it hotly.

It was on a visit to Toronto to promote *The Trip* that Peter conceived the idea that became *Easy Rider*. 'I was a little bit loaded,' he said in a *Playboy* interview later, 'and I looked at a picture that had been left on the table for me to sign for somebody's cousin. It was a photograph from *The Wild Angels* of me and actor Bruce Dern on a chop. I looked at the photo for a while and then thought about what it would look like if, instead of two guys on one cycle, I had each of the guys on a bike.' It would, he decided, be 'a story of escape, my own protest against all the hypocrisy of the current American scene.' It would include pot-smoking, a smattering of sex and Peter Fonda on a motorcycle. He noted his thoughts on a cassette recorder and quickly patched up his disagreement with Dennis Hopper, who struck him as the ideal director. Together they formed a production company and set about raising money for the project. Peter was still engaged on this when he visited Jane on the set of *Barbarella* and enlisted the aid of Terry Southern, the author of the erotic satire *Candy* and one of numerous screenwriters working on Vadim's sexual epic. The script, however, was unfinished by the time shooting began in February 1968, to coincide with New Orleans' Mardi Gras which formed the background to a vital sequence. In the event Peter was obliged to commit large amounts of his own resources, as well as forgo a personal fee, to get the film underway.

It became the lowest of low budget productions, shot on sixteen millimetre film and employing family and friends as cast members; they included Peter's own two children, Bridget and Justin, then aged five and two, respectively. The final bill came to $375,000, a niggardly sum in film-making terms. The film's profits were to exceed sixty million dollars and in a distribution deal with Columbia Pictures, Peter, as leading man, producer and co-writer, received a generous twenty-two per cent – an indication of the kind of film the company believed it had acquired. The award of a Best First Work prize at the 1969 Cannes Film Festival, not to mention a standing ovation, was their first indication that *Easy Rider* was something more than a Corman-style 'quickie'.

On the face of it the story was simplicity itself. Two drop-outs, the coolly detached Captain America (Fonda) and his freaked-out companion, Billy (Hooper), raise cash by smuggling cocaine across the Mexican border and embark on a trans-American odyssey from California to New Orleans. En route they encounter friendly hippies and deeply hostile Rednecks, two of whom blast the heroes from their motorcycles in an end scene of sudden and gratuitous violence. The dialogue was minimal, its place taken by an apposite selection of rock music.

Yet for all its apparent opacity, the film, more than any other in the sixties, captured the spirit of alienated youth and the backlash of prejudice and violence that alienation provoked among the more 'straight' elements of society. Fonda and Hopper's motorcycle journey was both richly thematic and portrayed with the rawness and clarity of documentary. In a series of telling contrasts it creates a picture of an America obsessed and riven by a desire for freedom, setting the often foolish idealism of the hippy commune against the unreasoning fear of Redneck reaction. As Jack Nicholson's drunken and friendly lawyer explains to the heroes: 'What you represent to them is freedom.' 'What the hell's wrong with freedom, man?' Billy asks. 'That's what it's all about.' 'Oh yeah, that's right – that's what it's all about, all right,' the lawyer agrees. 'But talking about it and being it – that's two different things. I mean, it's real hard to be free when you are bought and sold in the market place. 'Course, don't ever tell anybody that they're not free, 'cause then they're gonna get real busy killin' and maimin' to prove to you that they are. Oh yeah – they're gonna talk to you and talk to you about individual freedom, but they see a free individual, it's gonna scare 'em . . . it makes 'em dangerous.'

The heroes themselves act as a mobile sounding board for the attitudes they encounter. They follow their own dream of a hedonistic, pot-smoking, onward-travelling freedom, which leads to a dour meeting with two prostitutes in a New Orleans brothel, the induced madness of an LSD experience in a cemetery and their arbitrary killing on the highway. As Captain America or Wyatt (as Billy sometimes calls him – both heroes' names refer ironically to America's pioneer past which was forged by a similar breed of drifters and freedom-seekers), sums up their quest: 'We blew it.'

Hopper and Peter, in particular, did not so much perform their roles as
Overleaf: *Easy Rider* live them – and not simply by smoking real marijuana in the relevant

scenes, or having Peter in the LSD sequence re-live some of his deepest feelings about his dead mother ('Why did you leave like that?' he weeps over a female cemetery statue. 'I love you, God I love you . . . You're such a fool, Mother . . . I hate you so much.'). They lived their parts by embodying them totally, as Henry had embodied young Mr Lincoln or Tom Joad. As Peter said: 'I look at (*Easy Rider*) as my *Grapes of Wrath*. I don't say my acting was anywhere near my dad's acting was; it was a different style, a different stanza, a different piece of music, but it was still music. It affected an entire culture and it continues to. I have accomplished in my sweet, short life what most people connected with films dream of doing.'

He was perfectly correct. Not only did *Easy Rider* turn Peter Fonda into the single cinematic representative of an entire decade, a form of typecasting so indelible he has yet to recover wholly from its effect, but he succeeded in changing Hollywood itself. After *Easy Rider*, the film industry went in desperate search for more low-budget 'sleepers' which would give the same staggering degree of profitability. It opened the door to a number of directors offering a similar kind of hard-edged clarity and freshness in their vision, aimed at a new, young, critical audience – directors like Bob Rafelson and Hal Ashby (both of whom would also make good use of Jack Nicholson's newly discovered talent), Robert Altman and Peter Bogdanovich. All in all it was no mean achievement for a young actor-producer-writer who had yet to turn thirty.

PETER'S *Easy Rider* triumph both astonished Henry and made him extremely proud. 'Can you imagine Peter and Jack Nicholson and Hopper smoking joints and saying "Man! Man!" and capturing not only the mint but the reviews too?' he commented. 'I am in awe of this boy. He is more knowledgeable in a technical area of his business than I will ever be.'

Jane too was hugely impressed. She had encouraged Peter's efforts to get the film underway but no more suspected the end result than anybody else. At a stroke her young brother – whose irons she had always seemed to be pulling out of a succession of fires – had achieved the kind of success of which she still only dreamed. But the end of the sixties was to bring change to the lives and careers of all three Fondas. In Henry it was the least conspicuous but no less important for that. In his private life Shirlee continued to exert a steady and successful humanising influence. 'His whole life opened like a rose coming out from a tiny, tight bud,' commented Josh Logan's wife Nedda. 'Shirlee gave him confidence, and now he's even loquacious. He has a whole new personality.'

Both Jane and Peter, who had tended to regard their third stepmother with a degree of cynicism and suspicion, were won over. 'Shirlee is quite a remarkable woman,' Jane said. 'My father likes to play the hermit act, but Shirlee doesn't allow him to get away with it . . . His wives have had several things in common. They've all been blondish, extremely outgoing, very social, very effervescent, very energetic, and then he could tune out safely. Shirlee is the one woman who won't let him tune out.'

In career terms Henry was busier than ever, turning out half a dozen films between 1967 and 1969. They included a successful but hopelessly old-fashioned family farce with Lucille Ball, *Yours, Mine and Ours*, the story of a widower and widow bringing a total of eighteen offspring to their marriage; there were two taut police dramas – Don Siegel's acclaimed

Madigan, and Richard Fleischer's *The Boston Strangler*; and there were three Westerns. The first, *Stranger on the Run*, was also made by Don Siegel – as a television movie for NBC; it featured Henry as a drunken derelict pursued by a band of licensed renegades. *Firecreek* at last brought him together with James Stewart in a major role. It was a traditional, though low key Western, matching Stewart's timid sheriff against Henry's enigmatic and ruthless outlaw leader – ruthless enough to try to shoot Stewart down. If that were not sacrilege enough, Henry's last film of the decade, *Once Upon a Time in the West*, for Sergio Leone, the Italian Western enthusiast who had made Clint Eastwood an international star, went a great deal further. Leone, who lampooned the Western just as much as he lauded it, cast Henry as a kind of supervillain, who massacres an entire family – right down to its nine-year-old son – even before the film's title credits have been shown. It was a black joke Henry relished as much as the European, South American and Japanese audiences who flocked to see it – a chance to shrug off the straitjacket of decency and make a personal contribution to a fractious and iconoclastic decade. It was as if Henry were reminding audiences, and perhaps himself, that even in his mid-sixties he could, if he chose, be just as controversial as his two dazzling offspring. American cinema-goers, who clearly took their idols more seriously, remained unimpressed and stayed away in droves.

Henry's playful attempt to effect a temporary change in his image was no more than a hiccup compared to changes that were then taking place in Jane's life. These were to prove as profound and much longer lasting than anything Peter had experienced through the agency of LSD. In the simplest terms, it entailed a sudden and spectacular growth in political awareness.

In itself this was reasonably unremarkable for anyone living through the sixties, especially if they were under thirty. Both Jane and Peter now shared the hippy-style radicalism which concentrated on a necessary personal liberation – the best the individual could do was 'let it all hang out', 'do your own thing' or 'whatever turns you on'; these were all options that involved opting out in one way or another. Despite the uncertainty expressed by his *Easy Rider* remark – 'we blew it' – Peter continued to hold the same broad beliefs: love, peace and understanding between individuals would bring about the necessary changes in society, end the iniquitous war in Vietnam, usher in a new era of enlightenment and personal fulfilment. As the decade moved to its close, however, that kind of vague utopianism began to seem less and less viable. The heady sense of limitless possibility, of a new world creating itself, gave way to the shocks of the Martin Luther King and Robert Kennedy assassinations, the violence of the Democratic national convention in Chicago, the abrupt curtailment of the Prague

134

Spring as Soviet tanks trundled over the Czechoslovakian border. Utopia, it became clear, would not come about because large numbers of young people wished it. Society, just as much as individuals, would have to change, and that required political commitment.

Jane had not been politically unaware during the sixties. In 1964 she had visited Russia with Vadim, whose father had been a White Russian emigré. She had been pleasantly surprised. 'All my life I've been brought up to believe the Russians were some alien, hostile people sitting over there just waiting to swallow up America,' she enthused to interviewers. 'Nothing could be further from the truth. I was amazed how friendly and kind and helpful they were. My eyes were really opened to the kind of propaganda we've been exposed to in America.'

Working on *The Chase* she had learned about the plight of the American Indians from an arch-advocate of their rights, Marlon Brando. On the Louisiana location of *Hurry Sundown* – whose subject matter had provoked enormous resentment among local whites – she had witnessed racial intolerance at close quarters. Living in France for most of 1968 she had seen rioting students and workers demand extensive reform and bring the French government almost to the point of collapse.

But the focal point of Jane's political interest, as it was for many Americans, was the Vietnam war. Since 1966 there had been almost half a million American 'advisers' in South Vietnam, backed by an intensive aerial bombing campaign against the communist North. Jane was opposed to war on principle and was distressed when in 1967 her father visited Vietnam on a morale-boosting tour for the American forces; he insisted that he was still a liberal but that a first-hand view of the conflict had convinced him that 'a good job' was being done. When Jane tried to object he told her that she was unaware of all the facts. There was some truth in this and Jane began to take a closer interest in the subject. She followed Bertrand Russell's International War Crimes Tribunal taking place in Sweden, heard Peter's accounts of anti-war protests and draft card burning when he joined her in Europe to film *Spirits of the Dead* and listened to the personal stories of GI deserters who were turning up in Paris. Stories of the routine torture and killing of prisoners, of Viet Cong suspects tossed from helicopters, of random massacres of men, women and children. None of which appeared in official accounts of the conflict. They became an increasingly horrific revelation for her.

'In the beginning,' she said, 'it was very hard, very hard for me to believe what they were saying . . . I remember resisting, I remember thinking that I was brought up to believe that my country goes to war to help people . . . Eventually I was forced to face the fact that we were being lied to. Lied to systematically. Lied to since 1954 about American policy in South-east Asia.'

Previous page: *Madigan*

Then, early in 1968 as she completed work on *Barbarella*, a highly personal event brought her private and public concerns into sudden juxtaposition. At the age of thirty, she found she was pregnant. She was later to describe the birth of her daughter Vanessa on 28 September as one of the two 'most violently important things in my life'; the first had been her decision to become an actress. Her initial feeling on learning about the pregnancy was terror. 'I felt so vulnerable. I realised how I had always, strangely enough, rejected femininity because it represented to me vulnerability and a lot of things that scared me. During the process of becoming a mother I completely overcame this . . . I just realised that I am a female animal. I just came to terms with myself and my body and my fellow women. Truly my relationships with women have changed since then and consequently with everyone.'

This new awareness of her own nature had a political aspect too. 'I began to feel a unity with people. I began to love people, to understand that we do not give life to a human being only to have it killed by B-52 bombs, or have it gaoled by fascists, or have it destroyed by social injustice. When (Vanessa) was born it was as if the sun had opened up for me. I felt whole. I became free.'

Part and parcel of that new freedom was a release from the permissive philosophy of Vadim. Slowly Jane came to realise that the director's highly profitable emphasis on female sexuality imposed just as rigid a straitjacket as the stereotypes of Hollywood. It might move closer to raw emotion than Hollywood yet dared but in the process it focused almost exclusively on a single aspect of female nature, the erotic, and in terms that related chiefly to male interest. In future Jane would seek roles that provided more rounded female characterisations, and preferably set within a well defined and relevant social context.

There were sound career, as well as ideological, reasons for this decision. *Barbarella*, which reached America in the autumn of 1968, represented a fusion of Jane's still separate Hollywood and European careers – the American comedienne with the French sex symbol. As Pauline Kael's *New Yorker* review put it: 'Jane Fonda having sex on the wilted feathers and rough, scroungy furs of *Barbarella* is more charming and fresh and bouncy than ever – the American girl triumphing by her innocence over a lewd comic strip world of the future. She's the only comedienne I can think of who is sexiest when she is funniest . . . that innocent's sense of naughtiness, of being a tarnished lady, keeps her from being just another naked actress.'

Being 'just another naked actress' was a very real fear for Jane. Over a decade later she would keep a large photograph of Marilyn Monroe on the wall of her office at Twentieth Century-Fox – a constant reminder of the likely end point of a career built solely on sex appeal. As she was to say then, 'If I hadn't taken up a cause I could very well be dead like Marilyn. Not dead through drugs but dead just the same . . . I'd be a dyed blonde, a numb and dumb, pill-popping star.'

The role of Gloria in *They Shoot Horses, Don't They?*, one of an avalanche of scripts that followed the box office success of *Barbarella*, seemed to offer the very opposite of that prospect. Gloria was the heroine of a harrowing tale of one of the dance marathons of the Depression, when couples literally danced until they dropped in desperate pursuit of cash prizes. The story came from a book written in 1935 by Horace McCoy, a Hollywood screenwriter, and lauded in France as America's first existential novel. Gloria was a young woman embittered by repeated betrayal and brought to the edge of spiritual bankruptcy by the grim circumstances of her life. She comes to Hollywood with the dream of becoming an actress but lack of finance drives her to take part in the dance marathon. Its exhausting demands deplete her last reserves and she finally persuades her partner, a would-be director played by Michael Sarrazin, that her life is no longer worth living; at her request, he shoots her.

It was, in Pauline Kael's words 'the strongest role an American actress has had on screen this year.' Jane was well aware of this and committed herself to it fully, researching the background exhaustively and finally moving in to her dressing room because at home she would be unable to maintain Gloria's carefully built-up mood of negativity. 'I discovered a black side to my character I didn't know about,' she said. 'I became Gloria.'

The effort paid off. Though the film's depressing theme made it only a moderate commercial success, it was a critical triumph. Jane's performance was the finest of her career to date, throwing off for ever the mantles of *Barbarella* or *Cat Ballou*. She had become the serious dramatic actress she had always wanted to be. *They Shoot Horses, Don't They?* was her *Easy Rider*, her *Grapes of Wrath*; it won her the New York Film Critics Best Actress Award of 1969 and her first Oscar nomination.

But it had its personal price too. Long after the film was finished, the aura of depression Jane had established so painstakingly for her portrayal of Gloria still clung to her. It became entangled with her new awareness of the Vietnam war and America's part in it, the realisation that her relationship with Vadim was coming to an end, her fears that *They Shoot Horses, Don't They?* might have scuppered rather than rejuvenated her career (the awards did not come until the following year). She decided 'to go away and put myself in a totally new environment – in order to understand myself and what was going on inside me.' She chose India, following the hippy trail which had attracted large numbers of the young generation in search of enlightenment. The experience did enlighten her, but not into the love and peace mentality which Peter still professed. She was appalled by the abject squalor of the mass of the Indian population, disgusted by the indifference

They Shoot Horses Don't They?

138

of the hippies who lived alongside it. She flew back from Bombay to Los Angeles with a heavy burden of guilt, a fierce anger that her country seemed intent on imposing on Vietnam a form of colonialism whose after-effects she had witnessed in India, and an even stronger desire to do something about it.

Two events marked Jane's return to the States that November of 1969 and both underlined her dominant concerns. The first was the Moratorium against War, the gigantic peace demonstration in Washington which a newly elected President Nixon promptly and pointedly ignored. The second was the seizure of Alcatraz Island in San Francisco by American Indians protesting against racial oppression by the whites and demanding civil rights.

The Indians' cause struck Jane in particular. Here was a glaring example of colonialist repression much closer to home than India or Vietnam – three centuries before, her own ancestors had wrestled the Mohawks' territory from them in New York State – yet in kind it was not markedly different. She resolved to find out all she could about the Indians' plight.

Early in 1970 she got in touch with Peter Collier, a journalist who had written a sympathetic account of the Alcatraz protest in a glossy, left wing monthly called *Ramparts*. Collier accompanied Jane on a visit to the island where she listened to the Indians' case first hand and with a growing sense of outrage. 'I learned about the genocide that had taken place, that is still taking place, the infamies we had done to the Indians in the name of efficiency, in the interest of the white farmers,' she said in an interview afterwards.

The visit was the first public step in a transformation as profound as that of Jane's decision to join Lee Strasberg's classes, and a good deal more courageous. It began a year of the most intensive political self-education – a process that was to overturn almost every value and belief she had hitherto espoused, changing her life utterly. From a pampered Hollywood star, and an independently wealthy upper middle-class woman, she turned into a be-jeaned would-be revolutionary, rushing from debate to speech, from seminar to protest demonstration, lavishing her diminishing wealth on a bewildering variety of left wing causes, when not earning herself the nickname of the Mad Caller by constantly soliciting financial contributions over the telephone from friends and acquaintances. Her introduction to the American Indian cause also introduced her to an ever widening circle of America's New Left. She moved from the Indians to the militant negro Black Panthers to the GI Movement, which aimed to foster anti-war sentiments among servicemen, mainly through GI coffee houses set up on the outskirts of America's military bases. In March 1970 she first qualified as a fully fledged activist when she joined an attempted Indian occupation

They Shoot Horses, Don't They? with Susannah York

140

of Fort Lawton in Washington State. She was jostled by military police, who were a good deal rougher with the Indian protesters, and was eventually arrested. More demonstrations and more arrests followed.

There was no doubt of Jane's deep personal commitment in all of these activities. She immersed herself in the political counter-culture, the demand for minority rights of all kinds, and above all the anti-Vietnam war movement, with the same passionate conviction she had once invested in psycho-analysis and her desire to become an actress. But she had come to radicalism late and in her urge to make up for lost time her enthusiasm bumped shoulders with naivety and straightforward misunderstanding. As

Jane leaving court with attorney Mark Lane, after pleading not guilty to assault and pill-smuggling in 1970

her father's celebrity had once granted her instant Hollywood stardom when she was hardly prepared for it, so her own acting success launched her as a radical spokeswoman when she lacked both experience and intellectual background. As a result many activists distrusted her motives and regarded her effectiveness as questionable – with some justification: in November 1970 Jane's well-intentioned attempt to help some Black Panther militants led to their arrest by New Orleans police.

Though she could speak passionately and well about many of her causes, particularly her abhorrence of the Vietnam conflict, there was a vagueness at the root of her newly professed beliefs. 'All I can say is that through the people I've met, the experiences I've had, the reading I've done, I realise the American system must be changed,' she said. 'I see an alternative to the usual way of living and relating to people. And this alternative is a total change of our structures and institutions – through socialism. Of course I am a Socialist. But without a theory, without an ideology.' 'Socialism' was defined as 'a way of living where nobody can exploit the others and where the leaders are concerned about people and where there is no competition.' As a view it was as idealistic and utopian as anything her brother Peter had expressed.

But if the radical movement was in two minds about Jane, the Establishment, in the form of Richard Milhous Nixon, was not. As the Watergate hearings were to make clear, Jane received an inordinate amount of attention from numerous government security agencies from mid-1970 onward. Her mail was opened, her telephone calls monitored and in November, on flying home from a campus tour of Canada, she was stopped at Cleveland's Hopkins International Airport and her address book and vitamin pills confiscated from her luggage. She was also denied access to a toilet for several hours. When in desperation she tried to reach one – she was having a period at the time – she was restrained and arrested for striking a federal officer and assaulting a Cleveland policeman. The following day newspaper headlines announced that she had been accused of smuggling drugs. In fact the only chemical substances Jane had had on her were the vitamins and tranquillisers for which she had a valid prescription. It took over six months, however, for the charges to be dropped – largely because her defence lawyers tried to force the government into revealing why Jane had been stopped in the first place. They believed, rightly, that she was on a secret harassment list compiled in Washington; the government preferred to lose the case rather than make such a damning admission.

If the Nixon administration had hoped to intimidate Jane, its ploy could not have been less successful. The incident did more than anything else in her short radical career to convince her that her views were valid, that they did bite. She became more militant, more strident than ever before.

Henry was almost as upset by his daughter's conversion to radical politics as he had been by her public denunciations of him. He had hoped that her unconventional but apparently contented marriage to Vadim had brought stability to her life, especially with the addition of Vanessa. He had tended to dismiss her growing anti-Vietnam war views as yet another aspect of her natural rebelliousness.

When it became obvious that it was something more, they argued hotly. 'I told my father all the things I'd learned,' Jane said. 'He exploded, "You don't know what you're talking about! We don't do that. We're Americans. And even if the soldiers did do it, they wouldn't talk about it." So I explained to my father that when they start talking, you can't stop them. And he said, "If you can prove that it's true, I will lead a march to Nixon and confront him."'

Jane invited two Vietnam veterans to the home Henry now owned in Bel Air. 'They told him about the massacres, the tortures, everything. My father sat and listened very quietly, obviously moved. But he never went to Nixon and confronted him. He said sadly, "I don't see what I can do besides what I'm already doing – that is, campaigning for the peace candidates."'

By now, Henry, in common with the majority of American liberals, opposed the war but he did not see that as sufficient reason to attack the existing political system. 'I was fighting for civil rights before Jane could spell it,' he said. 'I'm not so much in disagreement with her sentiments as I am with the way in which she does things . . . She's a bright girl but she doesn't think for herself. She hears a second or third hand opinion about some injustice, and the next thing you know she's screaming revolution . . . I think she hurts her causes more than she helps them. . .

The Hired Hand She doesn't persuade people that *should* be persuaded.'

145

Fonda believed that Jane's new radical friends were exploiting her. Unlike their previous clash, however, he and Jane remained in close touch. Since leaving Vadim, she spent a great deal of time staying with Henry and Shirlee. Jane seemed largely unaffected by her father's comments – he was, after all, a representative of an older, more conservative generation who thoroughly disapproved of everything she had become. But she did show concern over criticisms voiced by Peter. 'It hurt when he told a reporter I get involved in causes without really understanding them,' she said. 'Why, Peter was the one who really turned me on to thinking about others in the first place. Now he goes around telling everyone I need to grow up and broaden my outlook.'

Peter's interests remained both more cosmic than Jane's and more individual. He was for ecology, against pollution, in which he included the mental pollution of prejudice, black against white just as much as white against black. He claimed to speak for no one but himself, his wife and his

Peter directing *The Hired Hand*

two children. His interests were split between an eighty foot sailing ketch, moored in Hawaii and bought from the profits of *Easy Rider* – and his film career.

While Jane spent most of 1970 rushing about the States in pursuit of numerous causes, Peter made a brief appearance in Dennis Hopper's next directorial effort, *The Last Movie*, and then set to work on a project of his own. It was a film entitled *The Hired Hand*, in which Peter both starred and made his debut as a director. A Western, it was a lyrical though rambling account of a drifter returning to work for the wife he had deserted years before. The critics praised the film's sensitivity, the performance of Verna Bloom as the deserted wife and the photography of Vilmos Zsigmond (who went on to win an Oscar for work on *Close Encounters of the Third Kind*); they disliked its pretentiousness. All in all it was a creditable rather than an auspicious beginning, but after *Easy Rider* Peter had a great deal of credit in Hollywood. He could afford to experiment as much as he liked.

With radical politics making an increasing demand on Jane's resources, she did not have the same creative freedom, but that did not mean she was prepared to be unselective in her roles. The one film she found time to fit into her hectic private schedule in 1970 boasted at least two of the criteria which had made *They Shoot Horses* so important to her: its theme, prostitution, had social relevance, and her role was a particularly strong one, a fully rounded characterisation which could only reinforce her reputation as a serious dramatic actress.

Klute took its title from the leading male character, a small-town detective, played self-effacingly by Donald Sutherland, who comes to New York to investigate the disappearance of a businessman and friend, Tom Gruneman. The central figure of the film, however, is Bree Daniel, a call-girl to whom Gruneman apparently wrote an obscene letter. Bree is highly successful but wants to become a legitimate actress and model. She begins a hesitant affair with Klute, falls in love and together they unmask Klute's employer as the killer of Gruneman, as well as a number of prostitutes.

The conventional thriller plot faded behind the glossy paranoia of Alan J Pakula's direction (later put to good use in *All The President's Men*) and the sheer bravura of Jane's performance. Her Bree Daniels is an intelligent and resourceful young woman who has made her own accommodation with an unsympathetic and male-dominated world. In her chosen profession she feels in control of her destiny, but at a high emotional cost – a numbness which her relationship with Klute both reveals and threatens. Her attempts to understand this process, presented in largely improvised speeches to a psychiatrist, are among the most powerful scenes in the film. And in common with the raw truth of those moments the story offers no easy conclusion: Bree leaves New York with Klute but there is no certainty about their joint future. 'It's not going to be setting up house for someone in Tuscarora, and darning socks. I'd go out of my mind . . . I've no idea what's going to happen. I can't stay in the city, you know. Maybe I'll come back. You'll probably see me next week.'

The film, which justly won Jane's first Best Actress Academy Award, was her last conventional Hollywood film for five years – at first because her increasing political commitment left her no time for or interest in mainstream entertainment, but later because of her unofficial blacklisting by a Hollywood grown tired and embarrassed by her unrepentant radicalism.

Politics now conditioned Jane's acting life. Early in 1971 she formed the FTA radical theatre troupe with Donald Sutherland, with whom she had become romantically involved. The idea of the group was to provide alternative troop entertainment to the morale-boosting efforts of entertainers like Bob Hope. Its initials were variously translated as 'Free Theatre Associates' or 'Free The Army', though every serviceman knew that it meant 'Fuck The Army'. Under considerable official harassment, the FTA performed anti-war songs, sketches and satirical diatribes outside military bases across America and at the end of 1971 went on a Far East tour where a film version was made.

It was Jane's most strident and fractious time. The loose consensus which had united America's dissident movements was now beginning to break up, with the greatest split between traditional socialists and activists who argued for a slow and steady process of change through the organisation of the exploited and those who demanded revolution now. Jane fell into the latter camp, with feminism joining her list of causes. It proved to be the most passionate and longest lasting of her beliefs; no small burden of guilt remained from her Vadim days as 'the ultimate sex symbol'. But veteran radicals disapproved the FTA for other reasons too. Not only did its work seem irrelevant – by 1971 few GIs went willingly to Vietnam – but the troupe was dominated by opportunists who hoped to advance their political and show business careers by association with Jane. These suspicions only appeared to be reinforced by the one film Jane made in 1971. *Steelyard Blues*, which was directed by FTA director Alan Myerson and co-starred Donald Sutherland, was an anarchic comedy about a band of social misfits who are constantly harassed by law-abiding 'straights' and plan to fly away to an unspecified better life in a restored World War Two amphibious plane. Jane again played a prostitute, the girlfriend of Sutherland who only becomes involved in his bizarre scheme when her association with him results in her being threatened by the authorities.

Jane's role was as lightweight as the film. It emerged as an uneven series of sketches, marked by an exuberant contempt for almost all forms of

authority. It was not a film radicals could take seriously or the cinema-going public of the day find particularly amusing.

There was no doubting the revolutionary zeal of Jane's next cinema venture, however. In January 1972 she returned to Paris to star in *Tout Va Bien* directed by Jean-Luc Godard. A leading and highly innovative 'New Wave' director, Godard had since become as politicised as Jane. Rejecting his early films he had vowed to make 'revolutionary films for revolutionary audiences'. The result had been work that not only submerged the director's considerable cinematic talent but almost entirely rejected the cinematic art as such in favour of the spoken word. *Tout Va Bien* was in fact his most accessible film for some time – though Godard's view of accessibility and the Hollywood-based view Jane brought with her were light years apart.

Jane played the part of an American television correspondent who visits a sausage factory with her husband, Yves Montand, a former New Wave director who now makes commercials. The workers they have come to interview go on strike and the couple hear both sides of the dispute. In the process they both become politically aware for the first time. Back home, however, it is made clear that this new awareness may have undermined their traditional roles as husband and wife; their marriage may or may not be a casualty.

The story was presented with many of the devices of Godard's new revolutionary cinema: direct harangues to the camera, prolonged and repetitive tracking shots, constant reminders of the artificiality of the film-making process.

Godard and his partner Jean Pierre Gorin intended the film to take its revolutionary message direct to bourgeois audiences, but its method still proved too intractable. It was hardly shown at all in America and fared little better in France, despite Jane's continuing popularity there.

The making of the film had been a disillusioning process for her. She had come to France lauding Godard's praises as a fellow revolutionary only to find that his directing methods were as dictatorial as any she had met in Hollywood and generally less sympathetic to the individual actor. But 1972 was to hold many more such disappointments. If 1971 had been characterised by internal wrangles in the radical movement, this year would set Jane at odds with the entire country.

The chief reason was a visit she made in the summer to North Vietnam, where she broadcast over Hanoi radio. Jane had been publicly advocating a Viet Cong victory since the previous summer, but this consorting with the enemy, as it was regarded, roused America's silent, and not so silent, majority. 'Hanoi Jane' and 'Commie slut' were among the kinder epithets from a mob that greeted her when she flew in to New York. She was dubbed a traitor by two Republican congressmen; she received an official

Previous page and right: *Klute*, with Donald Sutherland

150

rebuke from the State Department; there were calls for her arrest, which proved fruitless, largely because the United States and North Vietnam had never formally declared war. Jane, however, was deeply affected by seeing the results of America's prolonged bombing campaign, and she committed herself to the North Vietnamese people with the same fervency and the same tendency to gullibility she had shown with previous causes. It was a double blow then when Richard Nixon, the man she described as a 'cynic, liar, murderer and war criminal', was re-elected by a landslide in November, crushing his anti-war Democratic rival, George McGovern.

As soon as it was over Jane went to Norway to film Ibsen's nineteenth-century classic drama, *A Doll's House*. It had recently taken on new life as a precursor to feminism – to such an extent that a rival version was also being filmed with Claire Bloom in the leading role. This was hardly a good omen and matters did not improve as filming began.

The director was Joseph Losey, an expatriate American and former Marxist who had settled in Britain after being blacklisted in the McCarthyite purges of the early fifties. As with Godard before him, common political ground exacerbated rather than moderated differences; there was a fierce clash of personalities. Jane did not help it by taking along her own scriptwriter, Nancy Dowd, an ex-FTA member, and arguing for a greater feminist emphasis in the character of the heroine, Nora. Losey wanted the film to be closer to Ibsen's original spirit with a strong feeling of its nineteenth-century setting. Being the director, he won – mostly.

Despite the wrangles, Jane contributed a powerful performance – though to little effect. American distributors decided to take the Claire Bloom version for national cinema release and the Fonda version eventually appeared on ABC-TV. Neither version was a popular success.

But there was a bright spot in Jane's private life in 1972, and one that would have an increasing effect on her career. She met Tom Hayden who was to become her second husband. Two years her junior, he came from an Irish Catholic working-class background and had been a dedicated political activist since his student days. As such he had championed negro civil rights in the Deep South, become America's most conspicuous student organiser and finally achieved near legendary status among the New Left as one of the 'Chicago seven' when he was arrested for provoking a riot during the 1968 national Democratic convention. It was Hayden who had organised Jane's Hanoi trip.

They were married on 21 January 1973, shortly after Jane obtained a divorce from Roger Vadim, and moved into a modest home, which Henry promptly dubbed 'that shack', in Venice, an unprepossessing, oceanside suburb of Los Angeles. Their son, Troy O'Donovan Garity was born on 7 July.

Jane's views continued to make her unpopular throughout most of 1973,

153

particularly when she disputed stories of widespread torture in North Vietnamese prison camps as American prisoners of war began to come home. Another source of controversy was her championship of the Palestinian cause after that year's Arab-Israeli war.

But the tide of history was turning in her favour. American troops finally withdrew from Vietnam in March. Two months later the US Senate began its investigations of the Watergate scandal which would eventually result in President Nixon's resignation in August 1974. In a series of events that would prove to be some of the most traumatic in America's brief history, Jane's most vociferous denunciations of the regime, her most paranoid suspicions of governmental intrigue were shown to be substantially true. 'Hanoi Jane' had come home to a shocked and chastened America and to a Hollywood where 'radical' was no longer such a dirty word. But it would not be until 1975 that she decided there still remained a place for her in the industry which had made her a star.

WHILE IN the first half of the seventies Jane's acting career had followed a switchback, from the heights of *Klute* to a three-year silence after *A Doll's House*, Henry's had proceeded at a much more even pace. At an age when most men were accepting retirement, he showed no desire to slow down, driven – he claimed – by the fear of 'never being asked to work again, no one wanting me. Sounds ridiculous, but that's why I sometimes take jobs I probably should pass by.'

There were more than a few like that during this decade. For every *Sometimes a Great Notion* – Paul Newman's powerful film drama of an Oregon logging family in which Henry played a bloody-minded patriarch – there were poorly realised cinematic pot-boilers like *Tentacles*, *The Swarm* and *The Alpha Caper*. Cameo roles in films like *Midway*, *Rollercoaster*, *City on Fire* and *Meteor*, where he made another appearance as the American President, did little more than keep his name in the public mind. A second television series, *The Smith Family*, was only marginally more successful than his first. Based on the family and professional life of a rather lowly city policeman, this appeared in 1971 and 1972 when Jane was busy preaching revolution. It represented Henry's reaffirmation of faith in his country's institutions, though in the age of 'the pigs' and 'the fuzz' the choice of his screen profession was not a happy one. Cinema audiences were then cheering on Clint Eastwood's 'Dirty Harry' and Henry's sanitised patrolman lacked both credibility and dramatic impact, even for American television.

As he approached his own seventies, however, he did have the opportunity to make that reaffirmation credibly and forcefully in a series of roles that rejuvenated his acting career. The first came in 1974 when, after a five-year break from Broadway, he scored a hit with David Rintels' *Midway* one-man play, *Darrow*. It was based on the life of the famous American trial

157

lawyer, Clarence Darrow, a flamboyant character who had already been portrayed twice on screen, by Orson Welles and Spencer Tracy. Like Henry, Darrow had come from the mid-West and in a number of important trials had championed the liberal values which the actor had always espoused. Henry regarded the play as 'a beautiful conception' and made it, and the role of Darrow, his own. 'If Clarence Darrow was not like this,' declared the *New York Times*, 'he should have been.' The review urged 'everyone, man, woman and child interested in justice and America, to see this play.'

American justice provided the basis of Henry's next Broadway success four years later. *First Monday in October* was set in the United States Supreme Court where an elderly, crusty and liberal Justice crosses swords with a new, young and conservative appointee, who happens to be a woman. During a three-month run it broke box office records at its New York theatre, but it was to be Henry's final Broadway appearance.

The climactic performances of a fifty-year acting career were enacted on the screen – initially the small screen. In 1979 Henry starred in *Gideon's Trumpet*, also by David Rintels, the true story of Clarence Earl Gideon, a Florida drifter gaoled for burglary, who taught himself law in prison and sent a handwritten petition to the Supreme Court in 1962, eventually winning his own release. Henry regarded the character as the man Tom Joad might have become; in its last years his career appeared to be turning full circle.

There was a lot of the same cantankerousness and dogged determination in the role of Colonel J C Kincaid, which Henry played in April 1980 in NBC-TV's first live drama broadcast in eighteen years. Kincaid was *The Oldest Living Graduate* of a Texas military academy, the wheelchair-bound patriarch of an old west Texan family. The production proved so successful it was performed again on stage in Los Angeles. Awards were now being showered on Henry, prompted to some extent by signs of his failing health: in 1974 he collapsed after a performance of *Darrow* and was fitted with a pacemaker to correct irregular heart rhythms; in 1976 a large tumour was removed from his diaphragm; in 1979 he was treated for cancer of the prostate which had spread to his left hip; further heart operations followed throughout 1981 and 1982.

Honours came from both theatre and cinema. In 1978 the American Film Institute gave Henry a Life Achievement Award; the following year there was a special Tony Award for his achievements in stage drama; 1981 brought honours from the Omaha Community Playhouse, where the addition of a Henry Fonda Memorial Theatre would commemorate his name, and the award of an honorary Oscar 'in recognition of his brilliant accomplishments and enduring contribution to the art of motion pictures'.

Henry had always argued against the Academy Award system, claiming

Right: *Sometimes a Great Notion*, with Richard Jaeckel and Paul Newman Overleaf: *On Golden Pond*, with Doug McKeon

158

that it was both unjust and impossible to rate one kind of exceptional performance above or below another of a completely different kind. His ego, however, had never been small and while Jane's two Oscars had pleased him immensely (she had acquired a second in 1978), he was aware that his most successful cinema roles had not received the industry's supreme accolade. The 'honorary' Oscar did much to make up for that. As he accepted it neither he nor the Academy Award committee were aware that in a year's time Henry's name would be announced again, as the winner in the Best Actor category. His performance in *On Golden Pond*, in which he co-starred with Jane, was an extraordinary and timely event – not only a superlative display of acting skill which would provide a fitting climax to a long career, but a curious mirror image of Henry's troubled relationship with his offspring, a suitably public celebration of family by a family of actors.

But the film was not Henry's first cinema work to involve his children. In 1979, during breaks in the run of *First Monday in October* caused by illness, he filmed a brief cameo role as a bearded prospector in *Wanda Nevada*, a film directed by and starring Peter. It was a Western in which Peter played a drifter who wins fourteen-year-old Brooke Shields in a poker game and consequently becomes her reluctant guardian. Like *The Hired Hand*, it won critical plaudits for its visual eloquence but the inconsequentiality of the plot, and an uneasy attempt to fuse child-based comedy with overtones of Indian mythology (the Shields character is a half-cast) prevented it from becoming wholly successful.

Henry, however, was impressed by his son's skill as a director. 'He knew what he wanted, he knew how to get it, and everyone on that location respected him,' he said. He expressed as much in a letter to Peter: 'Your whole company so obviously worships you, and it's a beautiful thing to see. And I haven't seen it so often in forty-three years that it doesn't impress me.' It was rare praise from Henry, not only as a veteran actor but as a father who had not made a habit of lavishing praise on his children. Father and son were now communicating in a manner that would have been unthinkable a decade before, though the breakthrough had been largely at Peter's instigation. In 1976 in an otherwise routine phone call he had for the first time in his life openly told his father 'I love you', a declaration that reduced Henry to mumbling incoherency. Repetitions finally broke down emotional inhibitions that had crippled Henry's relationship with his children for years. 'What Peter did was good,' Jane commented, 'because you can't change yourself. Saints and prophets, maybe, but average people, and Dad's average, just as I am, you can't do it by yourself.'

Since *Easy Rider* Peter had had more than his fair share of emotional upheaval. In 1973 his marriage to the former Susan Brewer, which had survived the transition of lifestyle from country club 'straight' to

Wanda Nevada, with Brooke Shields

162

freewheeling hippy, eventually succumbed to the pressures of financial success. 'I was terribly upset by the divorce,' Peter said later. 'It made me a bit crazy and I knew I had the capacity to go off the deep end. I felt it to be a repetition of my father's life which I didn't want to happen to me. I thought I had failed. I drank, took drugs and was stupid. I felt being an actor, which I adore, would prevent me from having a meaningful relationship with a woman. I thought it would mean great sex and meaningless relationships, and that was very depressing. Success does destroy people, because when they become a tremendous hit they also become tremendously afraid – about money, for one thing.'

He survived by taking off, in a kind of nautical Captain America-style, in his Hawaii-based ketch, because when sailing 'you can't drink or take drugs. You have to be clear-eyed and clear-headed.' He also found stability again in a relationship with Portia Rebecca Crockett, a young woman six years his junior and the great-great-great-great grand-daughter of the legendary frontiersman. After a prolonged courtship they were married in 1976. By then Peter had abandoned his Hollywood home and the lifestyle that went with it; he now lived on a 161-acre ranch in Montana, a setting more in keeping with his avowed belief in conservation. There were fewer of the wilder, and frankly eccentric public declarations he had made in earlier days – he had claimed to be an anarchist and an atheist who wished to be buried, naked, twelve inches down in a simple hole in the ground, without a coffin, in order to 'give something back' to the earth. 'I realised eventually it didn't make any difference how passionately I spoke out about things,' he was telling the *Sunday Express* by 1979. 'People were going to go right on polluting the ocean and fouling the air. So I stopped talking about it and got on with my life.'

This statement gave evidence of a streak of realism which, as envious Hollywood contemporaries had pointed out, had allowed him to rail against rampant materialism and Establishment values while quietly amassing millions of *Easy Rider* dollars. In fact Peter had made concerted efforts to produce relevant creative comments on issues he regarded as important. While Jane was struggling to put a feminist perspective on *A Doll's House*, Peter was working on *Two People*, one of the first Hollywood films to tackle the subject of Vietnam directly. Peter starred with newcomer Lindsay Wagner – some three years before she became *The Bionic Woman* – as a Vietnam deserter who meets and falls in love with a fashion model. When they realise that, because of his situation, the relationship cannot prosper, he surrenders himself to the authorities. Peter was so anxious to do the film he spent months persuading the Oscar-winning director/producer Robert Wise to take it on. But for all its good intentions the script was poor and when the film was released in March 1973 it was savaged by the critics. It would not be until the late seventies that Hollywood succeeded in dealing with the Vietnam conflict, in films like *The Deerhunter*, *Apocalypse Now* and Jane's *Coming Home*.

Undeterred, Peter went on to direct his second film, *The Idaho Transfer*, which took up his favourite ecological themes. It was the end result of a project he had voiced in a *Playboy* interview shortly after *Easy Rider's* release: the plan to make a feature-length documentary on pollution. 'I want,' he had declared, 'to create an economic interest in ecology within the movie industry.' He had suspected, rightly as it turned out, that he would have to finance the film himself.

In practice the documentary idea gave way to fiction, though it was filmed in a documentary style using non-actors. *The Idaho Transfer* was a science fiction story set in a government experimental base where a technique has been devised to send individuals sixty years into the future. There they find a barren landscape which is apparently the result of some vast ecological disaster, whose sole survivors are small groups of moronic scavengers. Due to the physiological effects of the transfer, only young people below the age of twenty can make the journey. When the base is ordered to close down because of cutbacks, the scientist in charge despatches his daughter and a group of teenagers into the future to re-populate the world. Only when they are stranded there do they discover that a side effect of the transfer is to render them sterile.

The film's accurate depiction of the speech and manners of young people rooted the science fictional aspects of the story firmly in reality, but it also pushed matters close to the edge of banality, and occasionally beyond. That and a cryptic surprise ending – when it is established that there apparently are intelligent and still technologically sophisticated survivors, who fuel their vehicles with the live bodies of the morons – overstrained the patience of most audiences. It has never been generally released in Britain.

As both director and actor Peter has been dogged by the image of *Easy Rider*: 'People always tended to see me in the same way – as some kind of madman coming over the crest of the hill on a motorcycle,' he said in 1979. The great majority of roles he was offered in the seventies fell into a similar kind of anarchistic, anti-Establishment pattern: in *Dirty Mary, Crazy Larry* he was a smalltime racing driver turned robber, hotly and spectacularly pursued by police; in *Outlaw Blues* he was on the run again, as a talented but undiscovered Country and Western singer-songwriter, unjustly accused of assault; in *Futureworld* he was an investigative journalist, keen to uncover the iniquities of a corporation running a vast, science fictional leisure complex. Many of the films were in the American International exploitative mould which gave rise to *Easy Rider*: *Race With the Devil* was an efficient and effective variation on a witchcraft and devilry theme, harking back through *The Exorcist* to *Rosemary's Baby*; *High Ballin'* was a tale of truckers following hard on the tracks of Sam Peckinpah's *Convoy*;

165

Open Season, an updated Western on the violent vigilante theme popularised by films like *Walking Tall* and *Death Wish*.

At their most interesting some of these films were able to use the creative freedom of relatively low budgets to explore subject matter and approaches to film-making that would have been difficult further into the Hollywood mainstream. *Fighting Mad*, produced in 1976 by Peter's old mentor, Roger Corman, and directed by Jonathan Demme, was ostensibly another vigilante saga; Peter played a young city dweller returning to his country origins to exact revenge for the murder of his father and brother by an over-ambitious developer, keen to acquire their land. But it was both

gentler and more emotionally honest than the vast majority of its rivals and infused with a lyrical awareness of nature under threat from civilisation.

92 in the Shade, made the previous year and directed by Thomas McGuane from his own novel, was a genuine original – a quirky, if not entirely successful, tale of bizarre rivalry among boatmen in the Florida Keys. McGuane, who went on to script *The Missouri Breaks* for director Arthur Penn, tackles classic American themes in a highly individual and subtly subversive manner, merging scenes of sudden violence with wildly eccentric characters who spout dialogue that is as unexpectedly eloquent as it is hilarious. McGuane also happened to be both the ex-husband of Peter's second wife Becky and a close neighbour in a straggling Montana community which included actors like the late Warren Oates and fellow writers like Richard Brautigan. In the film Peter guyed his own image by playing an ex-exponent of Flower Power – and the scion of a wealthy family – who decides to make sense of a rather aimless existence by becoming a guide for fishermen. The story's mixture of inconsequentiality and significance, however, failed to impress American audiences and the film was never released in the United Kingdom.

Peter's difficulties in finding the right vehicle were matched by Jane's in the mid-seventies. The end of the Vietnam war and the resignation of Nixon robbed both her and Tom Hayden of a rallying point for their radical views. They decided that if they were to continue to work in politics, and, in Jane's case, in the cinema, it was time to make some attempt to come to terms with the mainstream of American life. To some of Hayden's activist colleagues this represented a sell-out – he had clearly been seduced by the publicity potential of being married to a glamorous and wealthy film star. But there were sound political reasons too. After almost seven years of highly vocal dissent, of mass marches and banner-waving would-be revolutionaries, America had had enough of unrepentant radicalism. Yet the traumatic events of the war, followed by Watergate and the economic recession, had badly shaken America's self confidence; once-hallowed institutions and well established habits of political thinking were now, however reluctantly, put under scrutiny. It was an apt moment to launch alternative but practical political ideas in a form that would be acceptable to the mass of voters.

Jane and Tom began by forming the Campaign for Economic Democracy, which aimed to represent the underprivileged minorities of California, from blacks and illegal immigrants to the elderly. Its policies included curbs on the power of large corporations and monopolies, the promotion of solar energy and the election of Tom Hayden to political office. It differed significantly from other, equally well-meaning left wing organisations by stressing that minorities needed to help themselves just as much as they needed help from government.

Fighting Mad, with Gino Franco

168

Establishing the CED and helping Tom prepare to run for a senatorial election in 1976 occupied Jane fully between 1973 and 1975. During this time she toyed with the idea of abandoning acting altogether, but decided it would be foolish to reject the mass audience to which her talents gave her access. Her problem, then, lay in finding films that corresponded with her own views. Her unfortunate experience with *Tout Va Bien* had convinced her that Jean-Luc Godard's form of cinematic agitprop was a dead end. The obvious alternative, Hollywood, was changing, but not fast or radically enough for her taste. Its film-makers 'don't view things socially and don't view things historically', she declared. 'Stories are unravelled in the context of an individual's particular personality and psyche and in the events of one life, never against a social background. You never see things dialectically which means they are lying to people. They lead people down blind alleys.'

As a result she began by turning down all of the scripts that flowed her way again in the wake of Watergate. They included *The Exorcist* and *Chinatown*. Towards the end of 1975, however, her views, perhaps modified by the day-to-day reality of her work with the CED, had grown more flexible and more self-critical. 'What is a progressive movie, what is a revolutionary movie? Is it really possible to make a movie that is a weapon for social change? I don't know,' she confessed to *Cineaste* magazine. 'I do have the feeling that, at this stage, in this country anyway, it wouldn't necessarily be a film that offers a solution. I have a feeling that there is a kind of frustration that may be progressive at this point. Perhaps the best we can do now is create in the audience a sense of hopeful frustration. Perhaps they should leave the theatre with a sense of wanting to move and a feeling that there is a good reason to move.'

It was a far cry from the strident certainty of her FTA days. Jane eased herself back into film-making by taking a small cameo role in *The Blue Bird*, a Soviet-American co-production directed by George Cukor. A musical version of Maurice Maeterlinck's fantasy play, it was one of the less fortunate results of detente. Jane took part as a gesture toward Russian-American co-operation and as a favour to George Cukor, who had helped her early career by casting her in *The Chapman Report*. It also gave her and Tom the opportunity to take a close look at the Soviet Union.

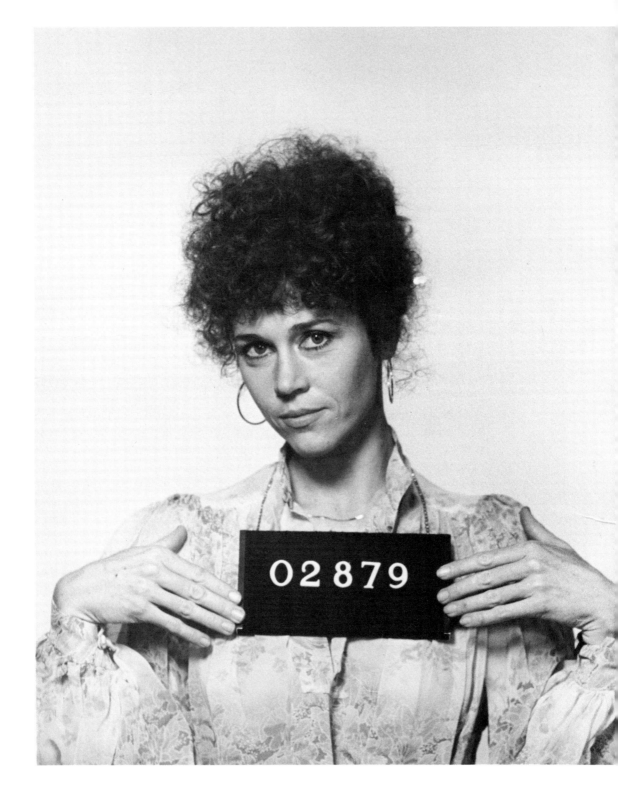

Late in 1975 Jane began work on the film that marked her return to Hollywood, and to cinematic success. *Fun With Dick and Jane* was a comedy, chosen, she said, to 'show that I could still be pretty and still had a sense of humour.' In its satirical view of American middle-class pretensions it also met Jane's criteria for revealing its characters against a solidly realised social background; there was even a marked feminist slant to the story.

Dick, played by George Segal, is an aerospace executive who loses his job as a result of the recession. Since he, his wife Jane and their son are living way beyond their means and largely on credit, this proves disastrous. Jane's attempts to become the breadwinner by taking up a modelling career prove abortive, because she has never been anything but a housewife. One day, however, they find themselves in possession of some stolen money and Dick conceives the idea of turning to crime. As unusually polite armed robbers they are an enormous success, though Jane gradually becomes the more daring and resourceful of the pair. It is she who engineers the theft of an illegal slush fund kept by Dick's former employer. For obvious reasons the crime cannot be reported and Dick and Jane resume their former lifestyle, though now on an even more affluent level.

The film was a critical and commercial success and restored Jane's credibility in Hollywood terms virtually overnight. Personally she was less satisfied with the result. Though the film proved that a critical approach to American society could also be entertaining, Jane felt that the story's most telling insights suffered from the continual need to raise a laugh. Furthermore she had built her American acting reputation on light, bright, quirky comedy like this and it hardly stretched her talents.

Her next film, *Julia*, seemed the perfect answer to all these shortcomings. Based on an episode from the memoir *Pentimento* by the

Fun With Dick and Jane

173

playwright Lillian Hellman, it followed the interrupted course of a passionate friendship between Hellman and Julia, a young woman who rejects her wealthy background to take up the anti-fascist cause in the Europe of the thirties. Hellman admires Julia for her convictions and her courage, which cost the latter her leg and eventually her life. The film's climax is the moment of Hellman's tentative commitment to Julia's cause, when on Julia's behalf she makes a dangerous train journey into pre-war Nazi Berlin, carrying thousands of smuggled dollars which will be used to buy the freedom of concentration camp inmates.

Impeccably crafted by the Oscar-winning director Fred Zinneman, the film reaffirmed Jane's talents as a serious actress, though the Academy Awards went to Vanessa Redgrave as Julia and Jason Robards as Hellman's lover, the novelist Dashiell Hammett. However, Jane again had misgivings at the end result. She had hoped to portray Lillian Hellman as a strong and independent woman whose life is changed by her warm, enriching relationship with another woman. In fact, Hellman's admiration of her friend was presented in terms that smacked of an adolescent crush; the playwright showed no signs of being changed by her experience of Julia and she was shown throughout to be almost wholly dependent on Hammett. Even the dangers of fascism were only lightly touched upon – Julia's struggles against the Nazis took place off screen.

The film did represent an advance for Hollywood by putting two female characters, and their relationship, at the centre of a major feature film, and its success gave rise to a number of films with a similarly feminist gloss, but this was not enough for Jane. The limitations of being simply an actress were becoming too obvious and too great. To make the statements she wanted it was clear to her that she would have to involve herself much more closely in the film-making process.

The means of doing so already existed. In 1974 she had set up a production company, IPC Films (named after Indo-China Peace Campaign), to make *Introduction to the Enemy*, a documentary on post-war North Vietnam. With Bruce Gilbert, a youthful veteran of FTA days, she now reactivated the company, and directed it toward feature film vehicles for herself. Unlike conventional film companies it would not initiate films on the basis of a saleable script or story; instead it would look for a relevant political point and then build a powerful and involving story around it. The formula for doing this was borrowed from *Tout Va Bien*, though without Godard's agitprop trappings. Typically the leading character begins by displaying a conventional and uncritical political viewpoint; then an event which arises logically from the sort of life she leads engages her emotions and causes her to question her values and beliefs for the first time; after an internal struggle she breaks through into a new and liberating awareness of her situation which changes her life. In the process the audience's

sympathies are also engaged and ideally they will leave the cinema with that 'sense of hopeful frustration' which Jane aimed to achieve.

IPC followed this formula strictly in three films which proved to be the most successful Jane had yet made: *Coming Home* in 1978, which won her her second Oscar; *The China Syndrome* in 1979 and *Nine to Five* in 1980.

Coming Home was Hollywood's first successful attempt to come to terms with the effects of the Vietnam war. In it Jane played Sally Hyde, initially the thoroughly conventional wife of a gung-ho US Army captain, played by Bruce Dern, who relishes the prospect of duty in Vietnam. While her husband is away, Sally takes up voluntary work at a veterans' hospital where she meets Luke Martin, an old school classmate who is now a paraplegic and deeply embittered by his Vietnam experiences. In an effort to understand and soothe Luke's bitterness, Sally befriends and then falls in love with him.

Previous page and below: *Julia*

176

All these events help to liberate Sally in a number of ways: away from her husband for the first time, she is forced to become more self-sufficient; in her relationship with Luke, a much more sensitive and attractive character than her too rigid husband, she learns something of the true nature of the war, and blossoms emotionally – it is suggested that Luke's lovemaking allows her to achieve her first orgasm.

When her husband returns, traumatised by his war experiences (with deep irony he has been decorated for receiving a superficial, self-inflicted wound), he is unable to face the fact of Sally's infidelity and, despite her assurance that she will try to save their marriage, commits suicide. A powerful and dramatically honest film, it also won an Oscar for Jon Voight as Luke and a nomination for Best Film.

The China Syndrome began as an attempt to make a film based on the true story of Karen Silkwood, a young laboratory technician who had gathered

Coming Home, with Jon Voight

evidence of serious lapses in safety standards at the nuclear processing plant where she worked. In 1974, while on her way to deliver evidence of her findings to press and union representatives, she was involved in a mysterious road accident during which all trace of the documentation she was carrying disappeared. IPC, however, were unable to obtain the film rights to the Silkwood story. In the tale that eventually appeared on screen Jane reverted to her Godardian persona as a television news reporter, though of a kind who finds herself relegated to heartwarming or quirky 'human interest' stories; the local TV company who employs her prefers male reporters to cover hard news, much to her annoyance. During a routine assignment at a local nuclear power plant, however, Kimberly Wells (Jane) and her photographer, Richard Adams (Michael Douglas, who also produced the film) film what appears to be some kind of crisis in the reactor. The utility company who own the plant claim nothing is wrong, but when Kimberly and Adams show their film to an outside expert they are told that the plant has narrowly avoided a reactor meltdown – the so-called 'China syndrome', when the nuclear pile overheats uncontrollably and melts its way through the bottom of the plant, theoretically all the way to China.

This discovery turns Kimberly into the investigative reporter she has always wished to become. She approaches the plant manager Jack Godell (Jack Lemmon), who has been alarmed by the company's indifferent response to the near disaster; investigations of his own have revealed serious flaws in the plant's construction, due to cost cutting. In a brilliantly portrayed struggle of conscience Lemmon shows the manager's personal ethics triumphing over his deeply ingrained company loyalty. Finally he tells Kimberly all he knows, but on the way to present her with hard evidence he finds himself threatened by company representatives. Meanwhile the plant is due to go back on to full power. In desperation Godell barricades himself in the control room and demands to be interviewed live by Kimberly. The company respond by bypassing the central control system and sending in a SWAT team to kill Godell, having convinced the authorities he is a dangerous maniac. Kimberly is unable to save him, and as the reactor goes back on to full power there is an explosion. A serious radiation leakage is contained, but outside the plant Kimberly interviews shaken employees, who now begin to admit that Godell was right.

A taut and superbly realised thriller, the film fulfilled all of IPC's broad aims. Not only was it an enormous critical and commercial success, but it had a galvanising effect on America's anti-nuclear movement, whose cause the CED happened to support. Admittedly this was due in large part to an extraordinary boost of free publicity when two weeks after the film's release in March 1979 an almost identical accident to the one portrayed occurred at

The China Syndrome, with Michael Douglas and Jack Lemmon

178

the Three Mile Island nuclear plant in Pennsylvania. *The China Syndrome*, however, confirmed Jane's position as one of Hollywood's most important independent producers and added considerably to her personal mystique as an individual of unusual prescience – the woman who had been right about Nixon and Vietnam was right about the nuclear industry too.

Nine to Five tackled the less explosive subject of the rights of America's working women, specifically office secretaries. It began as satire and escalated into freewheeling farce as three secretaries revenge themselves on their repressive and male chauvinistic boss, blackmailing him, kidnapping him and finally taking over his job when they prove they can do it much more efficiently. As newly-divorced housewife Judy Bernly, finding her feet in a male-dominated office world, Jane again played the 'transformed' character, though in a curiously muted way; despite her avowed intention to portray 'characters that are real to people', 'real' for Jane has never been interchangeable with 'ordinary', which Judy Bernly was. As a result the

Below: *Nine to Five*, with Dolly Parton and Lily Tomlin
Right: *California Suite*, with director Herbert Ross

acting honours went to Lily Tomlin's deadpan performance as a talented executive secretary, constantly thwarted in her desire for promotion.

With Country and Western star Dolly Parton making her acting debut as the office's unwilling sex symbol – and incidentally contributing a hit song to the soundtrack – the film was a potent commercial package, and became one of Jane's biggest earning films. But after the subtle and intelligent handling of important themes in *Coming Home* and *The China Syndrome* its comedy seemed too often gauche and obvious, repeating many of the mistakes for which Jane had once criticised *Fun with Dick and Jane*.

Not all her films at this time, however, were so obviously 'political'. In 1978 she contributed a bravura performance of sheer star quality to a segment of *California Suite*, the film version of a Neil Simon hit comedy play. She played a hardbitten, snobbish, East Coast intellectual disputing custody of her teenage daughter with her more easygoing screenwriter husband. The following year she scored another commercial success by co-starring with Robert Redford in *The Electric Horseman*. A romantic comedy, it dealt with similar themes to *The China Syndrome*, and in a similar way, but at a much less pressurised level. Redford was an ex-rodeo star, reduced to advertising breakfast food, who becomes outraged at his employer's treatment of a prize stallion. He steals the horse with the intention of returning it to its natural environment. Jane played an investigative reporter who tracks Redford down, becomes converted to his cause and enjoys a brief romantic interlude with him. The film was an entertaining vehicle for two superstar personalities, but its attack on corporate greed had nothing of the bite of *The China Syndrome* and its uncritical acceptance of the Redford character's advocacy of a half-forgotten, ecologically pure, Wild West heritage – as exemplified by the modern cowboy – was woolly-minded in the extreme.

More interesting, though less successful in both critical and commercial terms, were two films Jane made for *Klute* director Alan Pakula. *Comes a Horseman*, released in 1978, was an attempt to create a feminist Western. Jane played a small, independent rancher struggling to survive in Montana at the end of World War Two, beset by cattle baron rivals and an encroaching oil company. A bleak tale, it caught the hardship and dullness of ranching life rather too well, though it contained grittily authentic performances from both Jane and James Caan as the ex-GI who becomes her partner. For all that, however, the film's shoot-out ending was pure Western cliché, and as in *Klute* the feminist principle was undermined by having the hero save the heroine's bacon – whether she wanted him to or not.

Rollover, released in 1981, presented a similar scenario against a background of privilege and high finance. Jane was Lee Winters, an ex-movie star who successfully takes on her husband's financial empire

when he is murdered, apparently by a burglar. She forms an alliance, first business, then romantic, with a Wall Street whizz-kid, played by a miscast Kris Kristofferson. He, meanwhile, discovers that her husband died because he unearthed a plot by the Arabs to withdraw their money from the Western banking and investment system and convert it all into gold. This news is so momentous he is persuaded by the Wall Street establishment to keep silent about it, in the hope that the Arabs can be dissuaded. Lee, however, believes he is double-crossing her and breaks what little she knows of the truth. As a result the Arabs withdraw their money overnight and the Western financial system collapses.

However, the film failed to engage audiences' sympathies with the problems of the super-privileged, the intricacies of high finance which form the bulk of the plot, or the details of a romance which is treated so over-dramatically as to be occasionally risible. Following all this with the end of civilisation as we know it proved just too much, quite apart from being what must rank as the ultimate feminist put-down since Eve offered

Previous page: The Electric Horseman, with Robert Redford
Left and below: Comes a Horseman, with James Caan

Adam the apple: a lady financier's romantic uncertainties provoke the Apocalypse.

But *Rollover* was almost entirely eclipsed by *On Golden Pond* which appeared the same year. A former Broadway success, it was an old-fashioned story based firmly on the interplay of well realised characters and with no obvious 'political' overtones. It detailed the events of one summer when an elderly couple, Norman and Ethel Thayer, visit their lakeside summer home, probably for the last time as Norman is growing increasingly frail. Their daughter, Chelsea, a divorcee in her early forties, pays a call – chiefly to off-load her boyfriend's precocious thirteen-year-old son, while she and the boyfriend go on holiday in Europe.

Chelsea and Norman, a crusty, demanding man with a wry and savage wit, have always had a fraught relationship; Chelsea implies that she has not had children because her own childhood was so unhappy. Nevertheless she bears a strong, if unspoken affection for her father. In her absence Norman and the young boy, Billy, form a close companionship. When Chelsea

Below: *Rollover*, with Kris Kristofferson
Right and overleaf: *On Golden Pond*

186

returns she feels jealous that Billy has so easily done what she always found impossible. Her mother reminds her that Norman has just as much difficulty in communicating his true affection as does his daughter. When Chelsea attempts a reconciliation with her father, he responds favourably and a tentative but heartfelt mutual appreciation finally blossoms between them.

Jane and Henry had for some time been discussing the possibility of doing a film together; one project, which would also have included Peter, was a family saga paralleling American history from the War of Independence onward. When Jane, however, heard of her father's enthusiasm to do a film version of *On Golden Pond* she bought the film rights for IPC. Though the part of Chelsea was a relatively small one, she was convinced that the story's remarkable parallels with her own family's experience would make the film a success.

She was right. Co-starring Katharine Hepburn, the film was a tour-de-force by two of Hollywood's most respected actor-stars, and Jane's scenes with her father took on an extraordinary poignancy. Henry's Norman Thayer joined the gallery of his most resonant and accomplished characterisations – a fact recognised by the Academy of Motion Pictures Arts and Sciences on 30 March 1982 when he was awarded his first and only Oscar for Best Actor. 'I'm not a religious man,' he said beforehand, 'but I thank God every morning that I lived long enough to play that role.'

Jane accepted the award on his behalf: he was too ill to attend the ceremony. Just over four months later, on the morning of 12 August he died in hospital, while undergoing further treatment for his heart. There was, according to the instructions in his will, no service and no memorials: his leavetaking was in keeping with his acting and his life – quiet, understated, redolent of a deep mistrust of uncontrolled emotion. Characteristics any mid-Westerner could appreciate and applaud.

As MAN and actor, Henry Fonda cast as heavy and enduring a shadow across his children's lives as he did across the history of the American cinema. Its effect, frequently as traumatic as it was enriching, was to found an acting dynasty, whose star at the time of writing is as bright as ever it was at the height of Henry's career.

For the moment its luminosity falls mainly upon Jane. The former revolutionary has become a leading apostle of a new Hollywood orthodoxy, which grants superstars of the stature of Robert Redford, Clint Eastwood, Burt Reynolds and Barbra Streisand an unprecedented degree of freedom in choosing the films they make and the way in which they are made. With her radical principles tempered by political reality, yet apparently untarnished, Jane takes the responsibility of that position perhaps most seriously of all.

'Movies are so important,' she said in 1983. 'They shape our ideas and attitudes, even for we adults, much more than we think. And with more leisure time, more technology in and out of the home, what we watch will become very significant. I love being a part of that . . . I want nothing less than to help re-shape Hollywood and its depictions of human beings and their functions.'

Jane's creative interests continue to expand – most recently into television. With Bruce Gilbert she set up a highly successful situation comedy series based on *Nine to Five*. During a two-year absence from the cinema screen following *Rollover*, she starred in and acted as executive co-producer of her first television movie, a three-hour feature entitled *The Dollmaker*. Set in 1944, it follows the efforts of a young, working-class mother from Kentucky to keep her family together when her husband leaves the countryside for a steel-making job in Detroit. Joining him in squalid urban conditions, the family goes from bad to worse as the husband becomes embroiled in union activities and is beaten savagely by company thugs, and the youngest daughter is killed in a freight train accident. A strike then brings them close to starvation. The family survive by selling the wooden dolls that the mother carves as a hobby. One day a wealthy art dealer sees one and offers to pay well for all the dolls the mother can produce. Freed from poverty, the family return to Kentucky and buy the farm the mother has always dreamed of owning. The echoes of *Grapes of Wrath* seem clear and deliberate.

Meanwhile Jane's 'Workout' fitness studios – founded in 1979 as an alternative form of investment to the corporations she was often criticising – continue to flourish, as do the bestselling books, tapes and video films which propagate the Workout regime. Tom Hayden's career, too, occupies her energy and her finances – he was elected to the California state assembly in 1982.

Future film plans include a project with her brother Peter and it may well be that Jane's co-operation will bring the kind of fillip to his career that *On Golden Pond* did to Henry's – if, that is, Peter needs it. He, too, continues to work steadily. The most intriguing of his planned projects is to join up again with Dennis Hopper and make a sequel to *Easy Rider*, entitled *Biker's Heaven*. 'It takes place one hundred years after a nuclear holocaust,' says Hopper. 'This guy on a golden Harley comes down from outer space and brings Peter and me back to life to save America, which has been overrun by mutant bike gangs, black Nazis and lesbian sadists.' Whether or not such a bizarre project ever reaches the screen – and odder stories have – Peter seems content for the moment with his role as Hollywood's permanent outsider, forever threatening to re-take the film citadel with an alternative form of film-making that catches the mood of the times more accurately, and more entertainingly than anyone else.

Already there are signs that a third generation of Fondas could be entering the profession; both Jane's daughter Vanessa and Peter's daughter Bridget – currently a drama student in New York – have expressed an interest in acting as a career. Whether Henry's giant shadow can extend so far in terms of inherited talent only time will tell. One thing, however, can be guaranteed with more than reasonable certainty. The story of the Fonda phenomenon – its ability to entertain, to stimulate, to reflect a recognisable image of the world we live in – is far from ended.